WE ARE THE PRESIDENT

Maid in America

Daniel Washington

authorHOUSE®

AuthorHouse™
1663 Liberty Drive
Bloomington, IN 47403
www.authorhouse.com
Phone: 1-800-839-8640

First published by AuthorHouse 6/6/2011

ISBN: 978-1-4634-1460-3 (sc)
ISBN: 978-1-4634-1459-7 (e)

Printed in the United States of America

This book is printed on acid-free paper.

Because of the dynamic nature of the Internet, any web addresses or links contained in this book may have changed since publication and may no longer be valid. The views expressed in this work are solely those of the author and do not necessarily reflect the views of the publisher, and the publisher hereby disclaims any responsibility for them.

CONTENTS

First and for most I dedicate this book to God, for that was the way I was raised to acknowledge God who has guided me and protected me all of my life

To my mom, Dorothy Washington, who has taught me how to love and respect all women, She would sit me down and tell me the ways of the would From racism, to our relationship with God and to God as GOD with a name Y-H-W-H

To my dad Richard Washington who warned me of the dangers that I had ahead of me in life as a man

My dad, taught me how to work with my hands and to be thankful for the things that we have because there are allot of people who don't even have each other To the second most important female in my life, my wife Phyllis who stayed and prayed with me in life Who struggle with me as my loyal strong queen, my Conrad, my side kick, and my gift from the most high of whom I love with all of my inner being, and God forbid if we would have to ever part, she would be forever engraved in my heart

To my sister Christine Washington who was an image of my grandmother by her cooking skills Who has struggle hard to survive in a system set up to keep her oppressed, It has been a hard struggle for the black women
To my brother Richard Washington Jr who was died on Dec 9th 2006 who has always been honored to be my big brother

To my grandmother Evelyn Johnson aka Madea, who was a survivor in all circumstances who put a fishing pole in my hands and taught me how to fend for myself, who helped to raise me with all the love that a human can give to another

To my children who has loved me know matter how many times I've failed them, and still trust that if all fails that they can call on me to make things right.

To my uncle Anthony Johnson who gave me my first bible, and my first guitar, and always had faith in god, praying with me when I needed it, and taking the time to mentor me as a child
To my uncle Tim Johnson who taught me how to fight physically, mentally and to stay strong emotionally, who has always been a team player, for the home team.

The rest of the elders in our loving family Judy Lewis, Benny Johnson, Leon and Leonard Collins And to the late great Lemont Collins who was and is a great inspiration in my life.
to my cuz Shelton Lewis, who the feds got a hold of and won't let go, I miss you we have sheared some great times together
To my favorite knees Kenya Washington and her children of whom I love dearly, we connected at her birth and even though we have been apart in the flesh, we have always had a spiritual connection .
To my uncle Freddy Washington who always thought before he acted, and by doing so he achieved Just about everything he wanted in life.
To my uncle James Washington who has been married to the same women for as long as I can remember aunt Willie Faye who lives a peaceful spiritual loving life and raised their children to do also .
To my late uncle Winton, my uncle and my late uncle john Washington To my uncle AI, to all of my cousins from the Johnson to the Lewis's to the Collins family's And to my late God mother who has loved me all the time, birth Ethel June Forbes who came into my life at birth and loved me like I was her own .
To my great grandmother my mother's grandmother big ma, , my Indian queen,
as well as to my father's parents who lived in the days were a nigger was treated worst then a dog, but they made it through

these are some of the people who has paved the way for us And most of all to the slaves who gave their lives so I can have this great opportunity to right such a great book, for my generation and the generations after me can read, and grow from

I think you all

I would strongly like to dedicate this book on the most part to my big brother Richard Bubba Washington, of whom was born may 24th 1962 And taken away from us on Dec 9th 2006 My brother was the type of man that if you was hungry he would feed you If you was sad he would take your pain to make you happy. I

my Big brother bubba was 44 years old when he was murdered by the police department
He served 19 years in the state penitentiary, he got out and went back on a parole violation
He had 6 months to go before wrapping up a 20 year bid I remember when we was in Norfolk prison together, that he was going back and forth to the hospital
getting e-k-g work done on his heart .

He was the type of person that if you was hungry that he would feed you
He was a peace maker, if he had a problem with someone even though with his great boxing skills
That he would not fight them, he would rather talk things out and make peace
He held the boxing ring down in prison.

He was a big strong brown skin man with a lot of charm and character
He finally was excepted to a program in Boston called the saint Frances house .
I went to his graduation and every one spoke very highly of him
He showed me around and introduced me to every one
that's the last time I saw him .

My mom called my house and I will never forget the pain in her voice, when she said, jay Bubba is dead
Now it's unnatural for a parent to outlive their child
He was the oldest boy and all I can think about was the joy that my mother and father had when he was born
My dad was so proud that he gave him his name Richard Harry Washington Jr
I remember as a child 1 had a little jealousy because he had my dad's name, and my name was put together, with odd ball names, no one in my family had my name
My mom and my uncle Lou named me from my understanding.

But Bubba had my dad's name, the only thing that soothed that pain was that we called him by his nick Name.
We both spent several years together in the joint and we looked out for each other We got real close, the closest we ever been in our whole life.
And just when he almost made it to the streets again he was taken away
This is what I heard happened, even though he got along with the staff very well
They turned on him faster than a speed of light .

My brother had a problem with another inmate, and from my understanding my brother broke his foot off in some one, that turned out to be invisible, because when 1 investigated the situation the man could not be found .

Other residents said that my brother came down off of the elevator with someone else blood all over him
Then he went to the staff trying to explain his side of the story, the Boston police was already on their way.
Now this is the part that has everyone baffled, When the police got there, I understand there was a struggle,
if the police tell you to turn around and cuff up
and you don't move fast enough, they bundle down to the ground, choking and ruffling you up, and then
force the cuffs on you .
Now just for the fact that they had to take you down, normally a beat down came
once they got you cuffed up.

The word is that the police put him in that choke hold, and cut off his breathing, and with a bad heart it
was deadly force When they got him to the hospital he was face down and hog tied
They say he was D-O-A dead on arrival, just for the fact that my mother and father has to live with all this
pain is bad
So I will like to dedicate this book to my mother and father in memory of my big brother Bubba
Who wouldn't hurt a fly or let a bee die, even if it stung him

We couldn't find a lawyer to handle the case because most lawyers are afraid to go up against the police
department, or they want to make friends with the police to win other cases

So my brother just died, but will always be alive in our hearts for ever
And by putting him in my books he will live even longer
My great grand children will know there uncle Bubba
Dec 9th 2006 44 years old
Rom 3;23 Rom 6;23 Math 6;33 Rev 21;3-4

About author, my name is Daniel Washington
I am the author of a book called j baby, relapse and recovery
I am also the author of a book called outcast the ugly truth
I also have a children's book called poetry man
Order these books on line @ "http:, .www.author/"house.com

I have a great desire to be of assistance to my people
I am a man that has lived in the struggle, therefore I understand it
I came to believe that a power greater then myself, lives within me
And that power directs me to write the books I have writhen
I believe that as a whole, we need to acknowledge that no matter how much division we have
That as a whole that we are one
And there is power in numbers
SO WHO IS 'DANIEL J WASHINGTON?
I am you
I am the man that dreams for a better tomorrow
I am the man who is living in hell, looking to heaven
dreaming to escape to another place
I believe in change
I believe in equality
I believe in justice
1believe it took a lot of sacrifices of our ancestors
So we can have the blessings that we have today
I am you

Everyone from the first slave that came to America
To the last one free
To all the rappers disc jockeys and MC's

Hip hop has brought all cultures to hear the voices of our
Young as they expressed their selves aloud

To our James brown's urn black and urn proud

To our Michel Jackson's 'black or white'
To our Quincy Jones in the Motown fight

The 0 jays, the Delphonic's, Harold Melvin and the blue notes
The temptations, the 4 tops, Gladys knight and the pips
The whisperers, blue magic, black ivory, the mothers of soul Aretha Franklin and patty label
Smoky Robinson, and all the songs that they stole from little Richard

These are some of the talents that paved the way in the music industry
That brought unity

Songs that couldn't be denied, once you heard them
You can duplicate it, imitated it, but could never hate it

They bought together what was separated, and segregated
Yet even though they tried to deny, we still was singing the same old songs
From years of preaching and teaching
From the comedy acts of Richard Pryor
From the ministers in church
To the direction from the fathers
To the love from a mother
To the fast feet of Wilmer Rudolph
From the fist all black cast movie called a cabin in the sky
To good times, that's my ma, ma, to shaft and super fly
It took men like Barry white, Luther vendors, and Isaac haze
The Jackson five, Frankie Beverly and maze

It took our Danny Glovers, Denzel Washington's, and our Spike Lee's
The me- we of Mohammad ali

And in some cases
It even took our enemies
And we can even go as fare

as Langston Hughes
And Lawrence Dunbar

Harriet caring the load
On the underground rail road

Miss pitmen telling the truth of her day
And the story roots of Alex Hailey

From those who was innocent and found guilty in the kangaroo courts
Even those who was miss leaded and cheated
and became or best athletes in sports

From our bill Cosby to our Ophrah Winfrey's
To those singing mammy on their hands and knees

From the mama on all fours scrubbing the white man's floors
To the pimps, hustlers, players and street whores

To our Nat king Cole's, and Sam cooks
And let's face it, it took our black Muslims to
To stand up and pursue the work the black panthers wanted to do

It took the clothes we wear, the food we eat
Our style of hair, and the sneakers we wear

Music and TV entertainment and black actors
that played a big part in the acceptance of the black man

It took those that love us, and truly cared
And most of all
'IT TOOK A LOT OF PRAYER'
A LOT OF PRAYER'

It took the changing of hearts to realize that we are people too
And as the declaration said, 'all' men are created equal

It took courage, to stand and say,
I am going to vote for this strong well educated
Blackman
This African American

It took the participation of a nation
To elect an African American to lead the most powerful country in the world
It took a rainbow of all race's colors and creed

To finally realize that this was what this country needs

And today I can stand as a man, lift my head high and proudly say, we are the president
Heaven sent a& American made

THE WORLD IS YOURS

It's important that young black men check
Their history and have a good understanding of self
Who they are, Where they are
How they got here and where they would like to go
Have a good understanding of God
Gods will and self, Gods will for self
If you can crawl, you can walk
If you can walk, you can run
As long as the rivers run
And the earth is by the rain and the sun
As long as the stars shine from the heavens
As long as the rivers run to the sea
You can be whatever you wish to be
You came too far in life and history
Run and faint not
If you want success
All you need to do is
"succeed"
The world is yours.

"WE ARE PRESIDENT'
Heaven sent African, and maids in America

Y-2-K- NIGGER BLUES
IT TAKES ONE TO KNOW ONE

Nigger this, nigger that
When they gonna put nigger on baseball caps
Your mama never named you nigger
So why your boys call you that
No other race, at least to my face
Better not call me no nigger
It's a black thing, a figure of speech
That's what a young man wanted to preach
Nigger worker with nigger cotton sacks
Was once beat to death with nigger baseball bats
Chain 'em and hang 'em from the nigger tree
How to kill a nigger modem technology, the penitentiary
My brother - my brother "Why we call each other nigger?"
Sounding like the slave man with his finger on the trigger
Sound like the last word my great-grandfather heard
Before he was hung
I think it was "kill that nigger, kill that nigger"
We got one, we got one
One young man tried to preach
It's just a black thing, a figure of speech
Figure out where the word came from before you use it
Learn about the word before you abuse it
I read the Webster, Encyclopedia, Dictionary of the English language, the other day
And what I read just blew me away
The meaning of the word nigger
:A black person
:A member of a group of persons of disadvantaged social standing
"Second Class Citizens" "Second Class"
My brother - my brother, "Why we call each other nigger?"
You know we ain't no second class
Black people make up the largest racial and ethnic group of the United States
Blood, sweat and tears, worked the land for years
Made the foundation built to last
Nigger this, nigger that, nigger second class
When they gonna put nigger on baseball caps
Nigger t-shirts and nigger shoes
You can kill the nigger blues
In Y-2-K
From servant to slave
From nigger to negro, Afro-American colored people
In the next generation what they gonna call us then
Everything but neighbor, everything but friend
Why you call us that name
European slave traders, political and social race haters
You're the one who should hang his head in shame
You got my black brothers killing each other not knowing
Where they're going, from where they came
I charge you, you're to blame

The one who should bare the blame, the one who should bare the nigger name
So I ask you brother, "Why we call each other nigger?"
When no one is greater, when no one is bigger
When we're all in the same melting pot
We're not the second class citizen
Don't call me nigger, I'm your brother so call me friend
Know the game, learn the rules, let's kill the nigger blues
Do it for the next generation coming after you
When your children call you one, then what you gonna do
Our moral respect for each other should be much higher
Let's not feed into the nation-wide trap of the universal liar
Stop giving a hand to the Klan who wants Y-2-K to mean you to kill
Let's rise together, build together, layback and chill
So the resolution for this year should be to know the game
Learn the rules and get out of the habit of misusing the word nigger
There's other words to use
We must prove to ourselves, our colleagues, that we're not the nigger
That they expect us to be
The choice is yours what vocabulary to use
You can say brother and be at peace with each other
And in Y-2-K you can kill the nigger blues
Your standards should be much higher
Your demands should be much bigger
Than to settle for less adding to this second class mess
Because it takes a nigger to call a nigger, a nigger.

about book
Most people are simply tired of hearing about racism and hate crimes, and most of all, 'slavery.'
This book is to up lift all races, to raise the esteem of children who grew up around all others
Who came before them, in this unjust system of things

I hope it educates, mentors, and gives hope.
To make one look into the mirror and ask your self
Who am I?, what am I?, and were did I come from?
And the biggest question to ask your self should be
WHAT IS A NIGGER? and am l one

And who cares
This book is about the struggles that we have and are going through as humans
In a world of corruption and greed
This book tells the story of generations off niggers, Negroes, colored, black, and African American people
How they overcame the long standing grievances and massive injustices in America
Despite the abolition of slavery at the end of the civil war
But the never ending battles we still have to concur today
For the need for to express needs to be met and oppression of blacks be ended immediately
A demand for the right to live, by revolutionary ideology and by the commitment of the members of all races
To promote its agenda for fundamental change in America
For we as a people have overcome our differences and now we can have the same visions
'change we can '
Bull whip and beat a slave
Willy lynched in diabolical ways
Of weakening the mind and strengthening the body
We suffer yet never die
That which didn't kill us
Only made us stronger
We live through our children
Therefore we live
Through generations of our selves
God is the power that shapes our way
And our feet are set on a path that we may follow
When you are finished reading this book
I hope that you would have the understanding that
We are living in the beginning of a time of justice, liberty, and equality, for all
That our children and their children, will live to see that day,
that day our forefathers prayed for and dreamed about
It was there heaven, it is our reality
We are the trophies of the forbidden people
Who once had a dream
That all men will one day
Be treated equal
That you will understand that it wasn't just one man, that has been elected
But it is all people, from all generations

Who carry the burdens of holding the responsibility of making today, a better day for all mankind If it wasn't for the struggles of our fore fathers and mothers, and our struggles as well, from those that died violently depressed and opressed to the one sitting and has sat in jail cells He would not be president, so we share this glorious day together In unity with all walks of life

THEREFORE 'WE ARE PRESIDENT' Heaven sent & made in America

In Loving Memory of
Richard Harry Washington, Jr.
May 24, 1962 - December 9, 2006

Bubba/Abdul/and Phil

IN LOVING MEMORY OF
RICHARD HARRY WASHINGTON, JR. MAY 24, 1962 –
DECEMBER 9, 2006

My Big Brother bubba
If you was never born
What would my life be like be

Like brothers
We stuck by each other
With love, peace, and unity

And now that you're gone
I know life must go on
With you always in my memory

My Big Brother Bubba
God only made one

And now that he has taken you away
I can only pray
That we as a family
Will have the strength, to over come

With no more separations
Through our frustrations,
Confusion and division

Let's start living the way
My grandmother taught us to live

She said, if anything ever happened to me
Promise me
That you will take care of each other

And look, we have been so distant
That we don't even know,
When each other is suffering

So, on this day, I pray
In Jesus name
That through my Brother
We can draw close to each other
And yet his death not be in vain
Bubba was a man
That showed more love than hate
Always willing to participate
He will sacrifice his self
To help someone else
And believe me
He will be missed

Bubba would have loved to see
The unity
Of us coming together
Supporting each other like this

My soul is grieved
And my heart is troubled
I'm constantly asking
God Why? Why?

It's hard to say
On this final day
As we put you away
Good bye!

I feel for my mother
And for my father
Because it's unnatural
For loving parents
To outlive their son

So in remembrance of Bubba
My Brother
Think of family unity
Let's love each other
Like we was taught by my grandmother
And may Bubba
Always
Rest in Peace

In a world, that has showed him
So much conflict
Racism, separatism, and miss judgment

The world, has increased, in its many wicked ways
And god, has given, us so much, evidence
That these are truly the last days

Yet, we as a people,
Wave the peace sign,
In the midst of the increasing
Religious wars and street crimes

Now we are, all, we got
In spite of the many obstacles
That has, pulled us apart

May this Day be a Day
Of reconciliation, and redemption

For those who are wise
For those who will listen

We know each other's trials
We feel each other's pain

I want to do it for my Brother Bubba
So his death won't be in vain

Ecclesiastes 4:9-12

Two, are better than one
Because they have a good reward for their
Hard work
For if one can raise his partner up
But how will it be with just the one
Who falls when there is not another to raise him up

We have been suffering alone
For far too long

Vs. 12:
And if somebody could over power
One alone, two together could make a stand
Against him
And threefold cord cannot quickly be torn
In two

Seek first the kingdom of God
For with God on our side
Who can come against us?

May this day, be a new day for us to
Come together, in unity
In peace, in love, in Jesus name

Then my Brothers death won't be in vain

Because my Big Brother Bubba
World sacrificed his self
To help somebody else

I've been down in the gutter with him
And we struggled
And times were hard
Most days, all we had
Was each other, and God
And times, when I been in pain
He's been a comfort to me

And this world,
Has given, him, years of bondage
And finally, my Big Brother Bubba is free

So in remembrance of Bubba
My Brother
Think of family unity
Let's love each other
Like we was taught by my grandmother
And may my Big Brother Bubba

Rest in Peace

Bull whip and beat a slave
Willy lynched in diabolical ways
Of weakening the mind
And strengthening the body
We suffer we feel pain
Yet never die
That which doesn't kill me
Only makes me stronger
I live through my children
Therefore I live
Through generations of myself
God is the power that shapes my way
There for my feet are set on a path
That 'I' may follow

SOME OF THE HISTORY OF THE WASHINGTON FAMILY IN RANDOLPH MASSACHUSETTS

This portion of the book is for our youth to know how difficult times was for black families even here up north. To also enlighten the generations of the Washington family about their forefathers, to educate those who take advantage of the little things we 'take for granted 'in our daily lives such as peace, love, unity and freedom some of us may ask ourselves "why do I do the things that I do?
If you look back on your family tree, you may find those of whom you take after.

<You will never understand who you are, without the knowledge of where you came from>

This is a generation of people who struggle through hard times of being miss judged and prejudged yet still held on to their dignity as a family, stuck together as a family, and had a great love for each other as a family.

The plights and the struggles that they have gone through, as they traveled along and dreary road to finally meet success.

people think success is how much money one has, but wealth is not measured by how much money one has, wealth is measured by what one has in his heart, not in his wallet you are about to read about some of the most wealthiest people, God has given us.

In feb 2010, 1 had the great opportunity to sit and talk with three of the last four of the six Washington men alive the elders in the family, who still reside in Randolph Massachusetts, James Washington, Freddy Washington and Richard Washington.

sometime in the 1800s George Washington crossed the Okefenokee swamp
allot of slaves crossed the Okefenokee swamp to escape slavery for freedom
some died and very few made it through, due to the fact that it was loaded with poisoned snakes and other deadly creatures.

The Indians would help the slaves through the swamp, the white man sometimes would chase the Indians to the swamp and they was never seen again, it was the most deadliest swamp known at that time it was also a place for bootlegging and moon shiners.

It was so bad that the law had a hard time finding people dead or alive in the swamp
to most it was life or death, they was either going to live if they make it through, or die trying
so they was willing to die seeking freedom, then to live in bondage.

A man by the name of George Washington crossed the swamp and made it from Georgia to Virginia
now 1am not talking about the George Washington that crossed the Delaware, that you call the father of this country, and not the farmer George Washington carver.

This man ran from the dangers of slavery, to the dangers that stood before him as a former slave, in his travels, to end up moving to a segregated town, and becoming a great man.

I don't know how George got his name, 1do know that it is his slave name, and like most slaves they took on the names of their masters.
following his family tree, he did have some family that actually worked for the president George Washington.

George Washington settled down in Randolph from Virginia with his son Edgar in the 18oos.
and history tells us what life was like for a nigger, Negro, coon, jigger boo, monkey, ape, darks, Boy, and all the other names they called us in the 1800s, and in life.

Gorge Washington's son Winton W. Washington moved to Randolph in 1911
they was one of the only black families in the town at that time, politics was trying to destroy the family unit of poor black people by their laws of hate.

Yet George, and his son Edger, was hard workers and achieved their respect by being hard workers
and through there hard labor they was able to lift their heads up, and stand as men.
Winton had six boys and one girl named Ida, by a young lady named Ophelia, her parents died at a young age and Ophelia raised her brother Fredric and her sister Adele at the young age of 14 years old.

Ophelia was a kind spoken well mannered hard working mother who loved and took care of her children with the love of God, she would always read the bible and teach it to her children.

They raised their children in the 1950s the best they could with what little they had
the mentality of mankind never got know better.
So they survive by means of their own vegetation and live stock goats and chickens, ducks and pigs depending on no one to take care of them, but God.

the boys would hunt in the woods for rabbit, squall and ducks, Ophelia would skin clean and cook what they caught.

Winton was a strong hard working hands on kind of a man, who would always tell stories of his passed, he was always teaching his children survival skills.
Winton taught the boys the difference of copper, iron, and brass, and taught them how to take these metals to the junk yard and get money, they learned that everything had a price to it, from wood to card board, even old turn clothing was to be sold as rags, he was a great entrepreneur.

The boys would even pick berries and go from house to house selling fresh berries
they had a dog named king, king was also part of the family.
They would communicate with king and he would respond like he really understood what they was saying.

His son James told me a story that his father told him, he said that his father had a black horse and a white horse, he would work with theses horses.
the white horse wouldn't go up the hill, so one day while he was working he got to the hill and the white horse wouldn't go up it.
So he took a board a hit the white horse on top of his head, once he did that he didn't have know more Problems out of that white horse, in fact the next time he got to that hill the white horse beet the black horse up the hill.

What was the meaning of that story?
Once the white man gets it into his head, that we can all succeed together, then maybe we can get the job done. I don't know that's just my opinion.

James told me that when he was 16 years old he was tall and slinky but well built and strong
that they really didn't know how much of good shape they was in at that time.
He would work so hard on the swill truck, that his face would be covered with white, from the salt and Sweat.
When Winton got mad at people he didn't like he would call them low down dirty skins
till this day people don't know what Winton really meant by that statement
we can only imagine that he was talking about the white man, now don't get me wrong the Washington men are not racist, but wise.
It took allot of wisdom to survive and stay alive during those days when it was excepted by white society to be hateful and racist toward black people.

The six boys was very popular in town, they was known as the Washington boys
there was also another Washington family that was not related.
they was so poor some people called them the holy family, due to the fact that there clothes had so many holes in them, 'yet they was hard workers and 'stood as men'.

The winter times were the worst of all, due to the fact of the cold weather, they was unable to grow any vegetation, and Ophelia stocked up on as much food as she could by canning and preserving what she could for the winter seasons.

They lived in a big drafty house, with only one wood burning stove, so they all would snuggle in front of that stove to keep worm, as soon as they woke up in the morning, there they went straight for the heat of that hot stove, the house had about 8 rooms and a bathe room, and as the family got bigger they would convert rooms.

They would hand clothes down from the oldest to the youngest, and when they couldn't hand the clothes down no longer or the clothes just got to bad to wear any longer, Ophelia would take the materials from the old clothing and make quilts, to keep the family worm.

Ophelia was a strong spiritual black women, who prayed and taught her children how to as well she was also a good cook, she was able to prepare, clean, and cook anything
Ophelia cooked so well, that when the kids went to school, the little white kids would trade their home made lunch with the Washington kids just to eat her home made salt pork and biscuits.
Ophelia raised her children with class and wisdom, Ophelia's parents passed away when she was a little girl, a little girl with the responsibility of raising her little sister Adele and her brother Alison also her daughter Ida Washington, who was the first black girl to graduate Stetson high school in Randolph.
She was a strait "a' student who can Wright short hand and was far more advanced than the other students and one of her teachers didn't want to pass her so she can't graduate but she did
how you gonna be a strait "a" student and not graduate ?
There was no black men to take her to the school prom, so the same man that sold her dad A 38 ford car took Ida to her prom.

And Winton Allen George Washington played foot ball for the same school, he was the one who named the Randolph high school foot ball team the blue devils.

Winton senior was a very hard worker, in fact some of the things he built are still standing in Randolph <plat forms and steps> ect..

He was a man of Horner, respect, and dignity, who took pride in his work
during the depression he lost a house, fifty years later his son Richard was able to purchase that same house, it would have made his daddy proud to see that day.
It must have been a honor for Richard to work hard enough, to raise enough money to buy a house his father lost during the depression.

.During the depression in the 1930s Winton refused public aid, he went to the town hall and was told that he can have what they called old age assistance, but he couldn't work to receive old age assistance, he said know and continued to work.
 He was a man who didn't want to depend on no one to take care of him.
 So he worked and took care of himself, besides it was hard to trust a government that showed know mercy for you.

The town couldn't get the first blanking light in Randolph to work, so they called Winton's brother Edgar to help and he did.
No one ells could put this light up, Edgar Washington put in the first blanking light in Randolph.

Winton was a mason, he also raised chickens for a short time.
He also drilled and blasted, in fact he was so good at drilling and blasting they gave him the nick name ' the blast '
People loved his wisdom, they would talk with him, he would tell things even about the Future.
On the job when other people would be talking about woman, Mr. Washington would be talking about the Bible, He always like talking about the bible.
Winton came to Randolph in 1911 his father George was already here, he came in the 1800s

during the war Winton worked in the ship yard in Hingham mass, after the ship yard he worked for a man in Easton putting up plaster.
Winton was self educated, and had many working skills, the pay wasn't the best but he had work.
He took the hand life dealt him and made the best of it, he ended up owning property and land.

< a man traveled cross country at a time when he wasn't even considered a man, bought land and owned property>
Winton drove a 1938 ford car
his eye sight started to fail him over some time, and he couldn't drive that good at night.

One night he was driving and he hit a truck and that slowed him down a bit, but he still made it to work and kept on working, 'and stood like a man'

He was a strong man, one day he went to work and someone ells was using his wheel barrel
he kept his equipment in good shape and he had the cleanest wheel barrel.
 so this white guy took his wheel barrel.
When he asked for it back they had a few words, the next thing you knew the white man was
laying on the ground on the other side of the room.
When the boss came in he said, what so, and, so did this .and every one said Winton did it, the boss then said
if Winton did it then why is his body way over there on the other side of the room,
Winton hit the man so hard the man flew to the other side of the room.

Political games was played to stop black men from making any kind of progress.
A man by the name of Stokes wanted to build a house for his family, and the town was giving him a hard time.
So they played there political games and wouldn't issue him a permit to build the house.

once he went through all of the red tape at the town hall he finally got the permit
after he built the house, he went to get some belongings to finally move into the house
when he got back to his new home to his surprise the house was set on fire,
These are some of the games they played to hold the black man back.

Not Winton he knew how to deal with certain folks, he knew the ins and outs and had good social skills
some people called Winton George as well, they gave him this nick name, not knowing that his father was
really named George Washington.

Winton and Ophelia loved each other so much that one couldn't live without the other
they struggled together, raised their children together, and lived a life 'together'

then in the late 60s, they had a house fire in Randolph, in one of the houses that Winton built, with his
own two hands, the one that they lived in, burnt to the ground.
I remember that day, it was a sad one.

Now Winton didn't trust banks do to the fact that he lived through the hard times of the depression
so he kept his life savings hidden in certain places like in the chicken house, and in other places in the house.

maybe sown in his coat or mattress, or he would keep some in his wallet, when his wallet couldn't hold
know more money he would wrap it with a rubber band to hold it together.

When the house burnt down he lost everything, everything he worked for all of his life
So his body shut down and he lost his memory, it wasn't that bad at first, but as time went by, it got so worst
that he didn't even remember his own sons.
I remember visiting him with my father Richard, all the time, when they would visit him at the hospital he
would ask them, which one they was, and after he would go through all of their names, they would tell him
which son they was, our body has a way of defending its self,
And a short while after that he died, leaving behind his seven children, and other family members

When Ophelia took sick from a stroke the boys would visit her all the time in the nursing home
in the 70s she died from a stroke
The oldest to the youngest; Ida Washington who married into the name of Williams;

Winton Allen George Washington ;who served in the united states air force, as a a-p, when the army
recruiter came to the house to recruit Winton into the army he was gone, he knew they was trying to
recruit him and he didn't want to go into the army, so before they came looking for him he was already in
the air force, he went to school for pipe fitting, and was also a butcher for several years
John lee Washington; who served in the u.s army and fought in the Korean war .
While in the war he sent money home every chance he got to help his family.
James said if it wasn't for that money that he believes that they wouldn't make it.
Freddy told me that he still remembers the day john came home from the war,
everyone was so happy to see him walking down that dirt road with his bags in his hands.
Winton prayed every night for his son, and finally he came home o.k. he was also a medic in the war and every one
laughed when Freddy told us that john came home and gave everyone a vaccination shot .

And man he told some stories about the war that would just turn your stomach, one of the stories he
told about one of his fellow troops, one man was wounded and couldn't walk so john carried him for about a
mile from the enemy line until they got to safety.
 once they got to safety john put the man down, just to find that the man was dead, so he took watches off of
arms mind you the arms was detached from the body,
He did this for some off his close friends, he would take the dog tags from the neck of dead
and put it in their mouth and then push their jaws tight so the body can be identified.
He was also able to recondition anything, he would take a old car and make it look and drive like new
I have seen him do some, unbelievable work.

Alison Charles Washington ;also served in the army and fought in the war, he was also a good boxer
he told a story about having to fight this big guy who was very good at boxing, he said the only way he
was able to beat this guy was to knock him out in the first round .
and that's what he did with only a couple of punches .
he also loved his musical instruments, and like all the other brothers was good at building
and fixing things.

James Lou Washington; became a union worker, he had the gift to recondition anything, from cars to
electronics, he had the gift to look at something and figuring how it worked, and fixed it
For all of my life, I've watch him work, and raise his children the best he can

Fredric Edmond Washington; owned his own trucking business, he also built his own house, and worked
very hard with his two hands.

He has always been a good uncle to me as well, it seemed as if the more he struggled, the harder he fought back to succeed.

Richard Harry Washington; own a construction company for many years, then went on and continued building many houses, he became successful in real-estate, he told me that when he didn't have the money to build his first house, that a family that they call the goodies, this family was friends with my grandfather and the whole family, he gave him the cash to help him build his first house, and they was white, he used that as a example that not all white people are bad people
I had the blessed chance, to watch him take swamp land left by his father, cut down trees, fill it, and build a house on it, today that same land has increased in so much value.
In facted it was on that same land where I learned everything I know about tools and working
all the men are very handy, and have great survival skills,
they all ended up making a comfortable life for their selves, and never forgot the rough times they had as children growing up poor, and being judged for the color of their skin by a white society

So they appreciated the things we seem to take for granted every day, the small things
like running water, new tools, the ability to apply and maybe work a certain places, to buy a house in a white middle class neighborhood .
To put on a suit and tie, not because you're going to church, court, or a funeral, to go out for dinner and sit were you want to and enjoy a good meal, without hateful looks, or maybe not to have to go to the back of the building of a restaurant to be served, or not being served because
your poor and black
to be able to go down town and get a haircut by a black barber, without having to travel to another city to find a black barber shop.
when they was young they couldn't afford a barber, so there father would cut their hair, and as they grew older they would cut each other's hair, or just cut their own hair,

In their younger years, the Washington boys of Randolph was tuff yet respected they respected there elders and the community, People also respected them for the good reputation that their father left.

know body messed with the Washington boys, they had friends that was white do to the fact that they was one of the only few blacks that lived in town, they knew there place a young black men.

They would play with other white people in the woods and stuff like they was the best of friends but when they got older they saw the same old friends like in the down town area with their friend or family and some of them would just walk on by like they never knew them.

If they would apply for the same jobs as there white friends they wouldn't get the job but the white friends would get the job.
The only jobs the Washington boys was able to get was the jobs know one ells wanted, like working on the swill trucks, trash men ect.. ' yet they stood as men'

In spite of all that was going on they stuck together and had each other's back, that's the way they was raised,
 Freddy and Richard and James demanded that I noted that not all white people was racist toward them, and treated them bad, but for the most part they was unable to go into their houses.
There white friends could go to the Washington's house but the Washington's couldn't go in there white friends houses.

they even watch out for their white friends as well, when there white friend had trouble with other white boys from surrounding towns like south Boston, Quincy act.

They would come get the Washington boys to protect them.

one time cars was lined up from fern avenue to main street in Randolph, with white boys from all over to try and jump the Washington boys.

They wasn't know fools they knew that they was out numbered, so they didn't fight, but lived to fight another day, they wasn't trouble makers nor did they start any fights some just wanted to get a reputation off of the Washington boys.

They was good auto mechanics and was able to fix replace and repair anything
they grew up poor and in order to have something, they for the most part had to learn how to fix things to have something.

They all stood over six feet tall except for Richard and john, but they has muscles and was strong
Winton was big and strong, yet kind and quiet, John was a fighter that took know mess from know one he protected his brothers very well.
Alison was quiet and dangerous, James wouldn't pick a fight but if one came his way he knew how to handle himself very well.
Fredric was the kind of man that would walk away from a fight but would get you later
and Richard would just bash you in the face on sight if you messed with him or his family.

Yet above all they was kind respectable loving nonviolent men, who knew there place as young black Men.
They didn't have know black girls to date in Randolph, so they went to a small city named Brockton about 15 minutes from Randolph mass, to date their own kind <black women>

The Washington men was very athletic and mechanically as well as musically inclined
they had many friends in and out of the community.

As time went by and they all grew up matured got married with families of their own
they all became home owners some even built their own homes, they all became hard workers just like their parents, the apple don't fall fare from the tree.

Winton married a lady named many she was a nun, until she met Winton, they had three children
Todd, Linda and Claire
he also met a lady by the name of lily Pearle who had
Winton Jr, Vera Ann, and Raphael

Alison married a lady by the name of Susan and they had three children
Amacka, Charles who we call by his nick name 'chuck', and Tania
John married a lady by the name of Anna and they had the same kind of love as Johns parents,
and they had John jr, nick name poopsie, Joseph nick name Jo-Jo, Kevin and Tania

James married a lady by the name of Willie Fay and they had
James jr nick name jimmy, Dianna, and twins Timmy and Tammy they remained married for over forty years
and still married till this day

xxx

Freddy married a lady named Sadie and they had
Fredric jr, nick name 'Ricky', Tandalier nick name tonda, and Darlene, nick name dolly

Richard married a lady by the name of Dorothy and they had
Richard Harry jr nick name Bubba, Christine nick name Tina, and Daniel j, nick name jay baby

Ida married and her name became Williams ;she bore
cookie, James, ann., George, champ, and john
champ was named after his father James who was a boxer so they gave him the nick name champ
cookies real name is Lillian
we all have behaviors and characters of those that came before us

The Washington men implanted work· ethnics in all of their children, and just like their father
they went on as hard working men teaching their children like their father taught them
handing the God giving gifted down to their children, they all became hard working family orientated
people, able to hold their heads up and stand like men.

Even to this very day the Washington men live on the land that their father bought and built on in
Randolph.
Not all of the Washington's are alive today, John is no longer with us, Winton is no longer with us
Ida and is no longer with us, champ and Richard Washington Jr is no longer with us
yet they will always live in our memories and in our hearts.

As I talked with James Freddy and Richard, they spoke about their loved ones as if they was sitting in
the next room.
Reminiscing on the old days as if they missed them so much even though there was allot of unfair
Racism, and separatism they had each other, and life was allot more simple.

I had the privilege to speak with John on his dying bed, I noticed how he had such a good humor about his death
so I just had to ask him, how are you still able to smile knowing that you are dying ?
he said that he knows that he is going to a better place
and this is the man that fought in the war, and came home having a hard time adjusting, he told some
stories of the war, that we had a hard time dealing with, let alone actually going through these horrible
things.
Winton Allen George Washington died on the bleaches at a foot ball game at Randolph high, he died with a
smile on his face, he lived his life with that same smile on his face, he was a big man yet kind spoken and
lovable.

Adele Allison Washington Jenkins moved to new York: and she died there, she had allot of good qualities
and was a well respected women.
Ida was able to live a good life with her children always by her side

My great grandfather George Washington is the trunk of our tree rooted by God
and from that tree, grew many fine branches.
And those branches are the six Washington brothers of whom I call my mentors
they taught me how to be a father, a husband, and a man.

Not just by the counseling that I have received from these fine men, but by watching them, I've learned

that the only way a man will succeed in life is by working with his mind and his two hands
for what he wants.
And as death shall knock on each one of their doors, I pray to continue hanging on to this tree until I am
a elder in the Washington family, with my cousins, the children of the Washington men.

And if I shall ever fall I pray that it is not for the worst, but to be the seed to start another tree to grow
beside such a great monument as the family tree of witch I came from.

I come from a family of hard working men and former slaves, my family worked for a man of whom you
call, the father of the country of the united states of America.
Most slave owners had to families, the white family, and the winch, or the black slaves they had sex with,
even had children and fell in love with.

my great grandfather carried his name, and passed it to his son, of whom passed it to his son
did I inherit the ways of my father's? 'yes' for we have become but laborers in a world that has never
excepted us as men, yet we are survivors over coming many obstacles
and even though at times we may fall, we dust our selves off, and stand, stand as men
with dignity and self respect
so we stand, as men. Strong African and American men   'MAID IN AMERICA

SOUTHEASTERN CORRECTIONAL CENTER

CERTIFICATE OF PARTICIPATION

Daniel J. Washington

has voluntarily participated in Group Psychotherapy for Men Who Wish to Work on Managing Their Anger and Aggression

from 6/20/96 to 3/13/97

*In recognition of your motivation, contributions and progress
this award is presented*

THIS 17th DAY OF November 19 98

J. TYLER CARPENTER, PH.D., ABPP
COORDINATOR OF CLINICAL TRAINING

DONNA G. COLLINS
DIRECTOR OF TREATMENT

Attended group therapy in MCI-Concord- 8/8/95 to 12/12/95

Certificate of Achievement

This certificate is presented to

DANIEL WASHINGTON

For participating in treatment at
The Norfolk County Community Corrections Center

Assistant Program Director

Treatment Manager

Norfolk
County
Sheriff's
Office

Bay State
Community
Services

July 30, 2004
Date

The AFRICAN AMERICAN COALITION COMMITTEE

An inmate organization at M.C.I. Norfolk Prison

On behalf of our membership, as well as other Inmate Groups recognizing
the outstanding achievements of outstanding women;

PRESENTS TO:

Daniel Washington

ON THIS 8th DAY OF FEB. 92K

AN AWARD OF APPRECIATION TO EXPRESS OUR GRATITUDE FOR THE SUPPORT
YOU HAVE GIVEN US AND OTHERS, AND FOR MAKING LIVES WHEREVER YOU GO
BETTER.

SINCERELY,

Gary B. Little
CHAIRMAN

James C. Morris
VICE CHAIRMAN

CERTIFICATE OF ACHIEVEMENT

Massachusetts Department of Correction

Spectrum Health Systems, Inc.

This is to certify that

Daniel Washington

has successfully completed the

Transition Planning Program

on this 30th day of *June, 2000*

Director of Treatment

Transition Planner

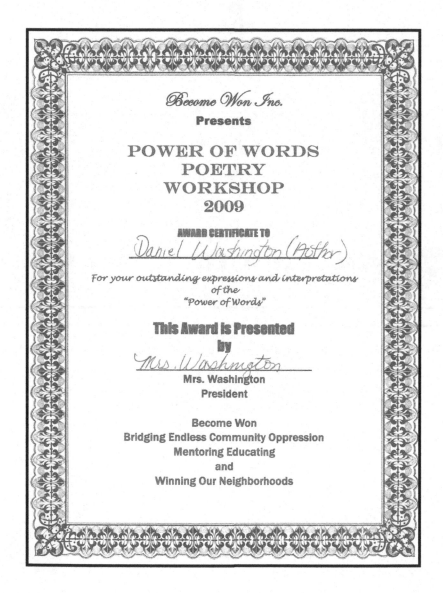

Become Won Inc.

Presents

POWER OF WORDS
POETRY
WORKSHOP
2009

AWARD CERTIFICATE TO

Daniel Washington (Brother)

For your outstanding expressions and interpretations
of the
"Power of Words"

This Award is Presented
by

Mrs. Washington

Mrs. Washington
President

Become Won
Bridging Endless Community Oppression
Mentoring Educating
and
Winning Our Neighborhoods

THE WILLIE LYNCH LETTER

This speech was delivered by Willie Lynch on the bank of the James River in the colony of Virginia in 1712. Lynch was a British slave owner in the West Indies. He was invited to the colony of Virginia in 1712 to teach his methods to slave owners there. The term "**lynching**" is derived from his last name.

[beginning of the Willie Lynch Letter]

Greetings,

Gentlemen. I greet you here on the bank of the James River in the year of our Lord one thousand seven hundred and twelve. First, I shall thank you, the gentlemen of the Colony of Virginia, for bringing me here. I am here to help you solve some of your problems with slaves. Your invitation reached me on my modest plantation in the West Indies, where I have experimented with some of the newest, and still the oldest, methods for control of slaves. Ancient Rome would envy us if my program is implemented. As our boat sailed south on the James River, named for our illustrious King, whose version of the Bible we cherish, I saw enough to know that your problem is not unique. While Rome used cords of wood as crosses for standing human bodies along its highways in great numbers, you are here using the tree and the rope on occasions. I caught the whiff of a dead slave hanging from a tree, a couple miles back. You are not only losing valuable stock by hangings, you are having uprisings, slaves are running away, your crops are sometimes left in the fields too long for maximum profit, you suffer occasional fires, your animals are killed. Gentlemen, you know what your problems are; I do not need to elaborate. I am not here to enumerate your problems, I am here to introduce you to a method of solving them. In my bag here, **I HAVE A FULL PROOF METHOD FOR CONTROLLING YOUR BLACK SLAVES.** I guarantee every one of you that, if installed correctly, **IT WILL CONTROL THE SLAVES FOR AT LEAST 300 HUNDREDS YEARS.** My method is simple. Any member of your family or your overseer can use it. **I HAVE OUTLINED A NUMBER OF DIFFERENCES AMONG THE SLAVES; AND I TAKE THESE DIFFERENCES AND MAKE THEM BIGGER. I USE FEAR, DISTRUST AND ENVY FOR CONTROL PURPOSES.** These methods have worked on my modest plantation in the West Indies and it will work throughout the South. Take this simple little list of differences and think about them. On top of my list is "AGE," but it's there only because it starts with an "a." The second is "COLOR" or shade. There is **INTELLIGENCE, SIZE, SEX, SIZES OF PLANTATIONS, STATUS** on plantations, **ATTITUDE** of owners, whether the slaves live in the valley, on a hill, East, West, North, South, have fine hair, course hair, or is tall or short. Now that you have a list of differences, I shall give you an outline of action, but before that, I shall assure you that **DISTRUST IS STRONGER THAN TRUST AND ENVY STRONGER THAN ADULATION, RESPECT OR ADMIRATION.** The Black slaves after receiving this indoctrination shall carry on and will become self-refueling and self-generating for **HUNDREDS** of years, maybe **THOUSANDS.** Don't forget, you must pitch the **OLD** black male vs. the **YOUNG** black male, and the **YOUNG** black male against the **OLD** black male. You must use the **DARK** skin slaves vs. the **LIGHT** skin slaves, and the **LIGHT** skin slaves vs. the **DARK** skin slaves. You must use the **FEMALE** vs. the **MALE**, and the **MALE** vs. the **FEMALE.** You must also have white servants and overseers [who] distrust all Blacks. But it is **NECESSARY THAT YOUR SLAVES TRUST AND DEPEND ON US. THEY MUST LOVE, RESPECT AND TRUST ONLY US.** Gentlemen, these kits are your keys to control. Use them. Have your wives and children use them, never miss an opportunity. **IF USED INTENSELY FOR ONE YEAR, THE SLAVES THEMSELVES WILL REMAIN PERPETUALLY DISTRUSTFUL.** Thank you gentlemen."

LET'S MAKE A SLAVE

It was the interest and business of slave holders to study human nature, and the slave nature in particular, with a view to practical results. I and many of them attained astonishing proficiency in this direction.

They had to deal not with earth, wood and stone, but with men and, by every regard, they had for their own safety and prosperity they needed to know the material on which they were to work, conscious of the injustice and wrong they were every hour perpetuating and knowing what they themselves would do. Were they the victims of such wrongs? They were constantly looking for the first signs of the dreaded retribution. They watched therefore with skilled and practiced eyes, and learned to read with great accuracy, the state of mind and heart of the slave, through his sable face. Unusual sobriety, apparent abstractions, sullenness and indifference indeed, any mood out of the common was afforded ground for suspicion and inquiry. Frederick Douglas LET'S MAKE A SLAVE is a study of the scientific process of man-breaking and slave-making. It describes the rationale and results of the Anglo Saxons' ideas and methods of insuring the master/slave relationship. **LET'S MAKE A SLAVE** "The Original and Development of a Social Being Called 'The Negro.'" Let us make a slave. What do we need? First of all, we need a black nigger man, a pregnant nigger woman and her baby nigger boy. Second, we will use the same basic principle that we use in breaking a horse, combined with some more sustaining factors. What we do with horses is that we break them from one form of life to another; that is, we reduce them from their natural state in nature. Whereas nature provides them with the natural capacity to take care of their offspring, we break that natural string of independence from them and thereby create a dependency status, so that we may be able to get from them useful production for our business and pleasure.

CARDINAL PRINCIPLES FOR MAKING A NEGRO

For fear that our future generations may not understand the principles of breaking both of the beast together, the nigger and the horse. We understand that short range planning economics results in periodic economic chaos; so that to avoid turmoil in the economy, it requires us to have breadth and depth in long range comprehensive planning, articulating both skill sharp perceptions. We lay down the following principles for long range comprehensive economic planning. Both horse and niggers [are] no good to the economy in the wild or natural state. Both must be **BROKEN** and **TIED** together for orderly production. For orderly future, special and particular attention must be paid to the **FEMALE** and the **YOUNGEST** offspring. Both must be **CROSSBRED** to produce a variety and division of labor. Both must be taught to respond to a peculiar new **LANGUAGE**. Psychological and physical instruction of **CONTAINMENT** must be created for both. We hold the six cardinal principles as truth to be self-evident, based upon following the discourse concerning the economics of breaking and tying the horse and the nigger together, all inclusive of the six principles laid down above. NOTE: Neither principle alone will suffice for good economics. All principles must be employed for orderly good of the nation. Accordingly, both a wild horse and a wild or natur[al] nigger is dangerous even if captured, for they will have the tendency to seek their customary freedom and, in doing so, might kill you in your sleep. You cannot rest. They sleep while you are awake, and are awake while you are asleep. They are **DANGEROUS** near the family house and it requires too much labor to watch them away from the house. Above all, you cannot get them to work in this natural state. Hence, both the horse and the nigger must be broken; that is breaking them from one form of mental life to another. **KEEP THE BODY, TAKE THE MIND!** In other words, break the will to resist. Now the breaking process is the same for both the horse and the nigger, only slightly varying in degrees. But, as we said before, there is an art in long range economic planning. **YOU MUST KEEP YOUR EYE AND THOUGHTS ON THE FEMALE** and the **OFFSPRING** of the horse and the nigger. A brief discourse in offspring development will shed light on the key to sound economic principles. Pay little attention to the generation of original breaking, but **CONCENTRATE ON FUTURE GENERATION**. Therefore, if you break the **FEMALE** mother, she will **BREAK** the offspring in its early years of development; and when the offspring is old enough to work, she will deliver it up to you, for her normal female protective tendencies will have been lost in the original breaking process. For example, take the case of the wild stud horse, a female horse and an already infant horse and compare the breaking process with two captured nigger males in their natural state, a pregnant nigger woman with her infant offspring. Take the stud horse, break him for limited containment. Completely break the female horse until she becomes very gentle, whereas you or anybody can ride her in her comfort. Breed the mare and the stud until you have the desired offspring. Then, you can turn the stud to freedom until you need him again. Train the female horse whereby she will eat out of your hand, and she will in turn train the infant horse to eat out of your hand, also. When it comes to breaking the uncivilized nigger, use the same process, but vary the degree and step up the pressure, so as to do a complete reversal of the mind. Take the meanest and most restless nigger, strip him of his clothes in front of the remaining male niggers, the female, and the nigger infant, tar and feather him, tie each leg to a different horse faced in opposite directions, set him afire and beat both horses to pull him apart in front of the remaining niggers. The next step is to take a bullwhip and beat the remaining nigger males to the point of death, in front of the female and the infant. Don't kill him, but **PUT THE FEAR OF GOD IN HIM**, for he can be useful for future breeding.

THE BREAKING PROCESS OF THE AFRICAN WOMAN

Take the female and run a series of tests on her to see if she will submit to your desires willingly. Test her in every way, because she is the most important factor for good economics. If she shows any sign of resistance in submitting completely to your will, do not hesitate to use the bullwhip on her to extract that last bit of [b----] out of her. Take care not to kill her, for in doing so, you spoil good economics. When in complete submission, she will train her offsprings in the early years to submit to labor when they become of age. Understanding is the best thing. Therefore, we shall go deeper into this area of the subject matter concerning what we have produced here in this breaking process of the female nigger. We have reversed the relationship; in her natural uncivilized state, she would have a strong dependency on the uncivilized nigger male, and she would have a limited protective tendency toward her independent male offspring and would raise male offsprings to be dependent like her. Nature had provided for this type of balance. We reversed nature by burning and pulling a civilized nigger apart and bullwhipping the other to the point of death, all in her presence. By her being left alone, unprotected, with the **MALE IMAGE DESTROYED**, the ordeal caused her to move from her psychologically dependent state to a frozen, independent state. In this frozen, psychological state of independence, she will raise her **MALE** and female offspring in reversed roles. For **FEAR** of the young male's life, she will psychologically train him to be **MENTALLY WEAK** and **DEPENDENT**, but **PHYSICALLY STRONG**. Because she has become psychologically independent, she will train her **FEMALE** offsprings to be psychologically independent. What have you got? You've got the nigger **WOMAN OUT FRONT AND THE** nigger **MAN BEHIND AND SCARED**. This is a perfect situation of sound sleep and economics. Before the breaking process, we had to be alertly on guard at all times. Now, we can sleep soundly, for out of frozen fear his woman stands guard for us. He cannot get past her early slave-molding process. He is a good tool, now ready to be tied to the horse at a tender age. By the time a nigger boy reaches the age of sixteen, he is soundly broken in and ready for a long life of sound and efficient work and the reproduction of a unit of good labor force. Continually through the breaking of uncivilized savage niggers, by throwing the nigger female savage into a frozen psychological state of independence, by killing the protective male image, and by creating a submissive dependent mind of the nigger male slave, we have created an orbiting cycle that turns on its own axis forever, unless a phenomenon occurs and re-shifts the position of the male and female slaves. We show what we mean by example. Take the case of the two economic slave units and examine them close.

THE NEGRO MARRIAGE

We breed two nigger males with two nigger females. Then, we take the nigger male away from them and keep them moving and working. Say one nigger female bears a nigger female and the other bears a nigger male; both nigger females—being without influence of the nigger male image, frozen with a independent psychology—will raise their offspring into reverse positions. The one with the female offspring will teach her to be like herself, independent and negotiable (we negotiate with her, through her, by her, negotiates her at will). The one with the nigger male offspring, she being frozen subconscious fear for his life, will raise him to be mentally dependent and weak, but physically strong; in other words, body over mind. Now, in a few years when these two offsprings become fertile for early reproduction, we will mate and breed them and continue the cycle. That is good, sound and long range comprehensive planning.

WARNING: POSSIBLE INTERLOPING NEGATIVES

Earlier, we talked about the non-economic good of the horse and the nigger in their wild or natural state; we talked out the principle of breaking and tying them together for orderly production. Furthermore, we talked about paying particular attention to the female savage and her offspring for orderly future planning, then more recently we stated that, by reversing the positions of the male and female savages, we created an orbiting cycle that turns on its own axis forever unless a phenomenon occurred and reshifts positions of the male and female savages. Our experts warned us about the possibility of this phenomenon occurring, for they say that the mind has a strong drive to correct and re-correct itself over a period of time if it can touch some substantial original historical base; and they advised us that the best way to deal with the phenomenon is to shave off the brute's mental history and create a multiplicity of phenomena of illusions, so that each illusion will twirl in its own orbit, something similar to floating balls in a vacuum. This creation of multiplicity of phenomena of illusions entails the principle of crossbreeding the nigger and the horse as we stated above, the purpose of which is to create a diversified division of labor; thereby creating different levels of labor and different values of illusion at each connecting level of labor. The results of which is the severance of the points of original beginnings for each sphere illusion. Since we feel that the subject matter may get more complicated as we proceed in laying down our economic plan concerning the purpose, reason and effect of crossbreeding horses and niggers, we shall lay down the following definition terms for future generations. Orbiting cycle means a thing turning in a given path. Axis means upon which or around which a body turns. Phenomenon means something beyond ordinary conception and inspires awe and wonder. Multiplicity means a great number. Means a globe. Crossbreeding a horse means taking a horse and breeding it with an ass and you get a dumb, backward, ass long-headed mule that is not reproductive nor productive by itself. Crossbreeding niggers mean taking so many drops of good white blood and putting them into as many nigger women as possible, varying the drops by the various tone that you want, and then letting them breed with each other until another circle of color appears as you desire. What this means is this: Put the niggers and the horse in a breeding pot, mix some asses and some good white blood and what do you get? You got a multiplicity of colors of ass backward, unusual niggers, running, tied to backward ass long-headed mules, the one productive of itself, the other sterile. (The one constant, the other dying, we keep the nigger constant for we may replace the mules for another tool) both mule and nigger tied to each other, neither knowing where the other came from and neither productive for itself, nor without each other.

CONTROLLED LANGUAGE

Crossbreeding completed, for further severance from their original beginning, **WE MUST COMPLETELY ANNIHILATE THE MOTHER TONGUE** of both the new nigger and the new mule, and institute a new language that involves the new life's work of both. You know language is a peculiar institution. It leads to the heart of a people. The more a foreigner knows about the language of another country the more he is able to move through all levels of that society. Therefore, if the foreigner is an enemy of the country, to the extent that he knows the body of the language, to that extent is the country vulnerable to attack or invasion of a foreign culture. For example, if you take a slave, if you teach him all about your language, he will know all your secrets, and he is then no more a slave, for you can't fool him any longer, and **BEING A FOOL IS ONE OF THE BASIC INGREDIENTS OF ANY INCIDENTS TO THE MAINTENANCE OF THE SLAVERY SYSTEM**. For example, if you told a slave that he must perform in getting out "our crops" and he knows the language well, he would know that "our crops" didn't mean "our crops" and the slavery system would break down, for he would relate on the basis of what "our crops" really meant. So you have to be careful in setting up the new language; for the slaves would soon be in your house, talking to you as "man to man" and that is death to our economic system. In addition, the definitions of words or terms are only a minute part of the process. Values are created and transported by communication through the body of the language. A total society has many interconnected value systems. All the values in the society have bridges of language to connect them for orderly working in the society. But for these language bridges, these many value systems would sharply clash and cause internal strife or civil war, the degree of the conflict being determined by the magnitude of the issues or relative opposing strength in whatever form. For example, if you put a slave in a hog pen and train him to live there and incorporate in him to value it as a way of life completely, the biggest problem you would have out of him is that he would worry you about provisions to keep the hog pen clean, or the same hog pen and make a slip and incorporate something in his language whereby he comes to value a house more than he does his hog pen, you got a problem. He will soon be in your house.

CHAPTER 1: AMERICA THE HOME OF THE RICH

DESTRUCTION

<u>Title</u>
Uncleanness-Depression-Discouragement-Defeat-Jealousy-Criticism-JudgementDestruction

<u>Text</u>
Matthew 12:43-45

<u>Introduction</u>
Jesus told the story of a "man" who had gotten saved.
He also talked about how the devil
Had to get out when the man got saved
I call this man, "BLACK MAN'

If we could pull the curtain back and see beyond
The physical realm. We will witness the diabolical scene.
Picture if you will ....

The unclean spirit goes to a convention of demons
He has found no rest outside of Black Man
The body of which he once lived in
The unclean spirit tries to sneak out of the convention
As Lucifer stands screaming at the demons
Flaming fingers in his direction, fiery arrows
Aimed at the demons
Satan says "What are you doing here, U clean?"
"I thought I sent you to possess Black Man?"
"Give me an account of yourself
It better be good".
Now every wicked spirit is looking at Unclean
As he shakes with fear and speaks with a
Trembling voice
I was living in Black Man for years
I had him doing drugs, lying, stealing
And doing every unclean thing I made him do
Until Sunday when he went to church in prison
And accepted Jesus into his heart
Satan yells with a violent rage until all Hell shakes
"Don't ever say that name again in my presence
I hate it, I hate it"
As the brimstone walls glow with reflected fire
Another demon stands up
My name is "Discouragement" I will go with
Unclean to visit Black Man. I will work a
Few things to make him Discouraged.
I'll just have someone from his church go to
The new pastor and say nasty things about him.
Another demon stands to speak
My name is "Depression", I'll go with Unclean and

1

Discouragement. I'll make him feel as if he is
Not wanted in the church because he's black and
I'll make him feel less than depressed.
A third demon stands, my name is "Defeat"
I've worked a lot of churches and people like Black Man.
I'll go when things are at a low point
I'll take a brother from the church who works
With him on his job and have him snitching
Other people out and lying on others for a very
Small raise. When Black Man sees this he will
Leave the job, church and be defeated.
Excitement is starting to build.
The fourth demon jumps to his feet and claps
His hands with glee.
My name is "Jealousy", when Discouragement, Depression
And Defeat go with Unclean, let me go too.
When Black Man gets really defeated and starts
Taking a look around the church
I'll show him all of the back stabbing snitches
Who make more trouble than disciple's in the church
Those who would do anything to be choir director or
Guitar player. I'll have him looking at other
People instead of the Word of God.
I'll have him complaining about the position in the church
That other people who have not even been
Called by God or anointed by God
I'll make him so jealous he won't ever get over it
The fifth demon jumps up. My name is "Criticism"
And I want to go.
I'll get him to start criticizing just a little bit
With just a little sarcasm.
Pretty soon he'll be attacking everybody
Of course, I'll make sure some people criticize
Him too.
What's good for sin is good for the sinner
The sixth demon stands to offer his services
I'm the spirit of "Judgment"
After Black Man has been overcome by criticism
I'll cause him to start passing judgment on them
Like never before
I'll even make him say the whole church are nothing
But hypocrites
And they need to go straight to where we are if you
Know what I mean?
Finally a big sour looking demon pulls himself
Up into a hateful, steady, seasoned voice
He begins to speak
My name is "Destruction"
The plan of action against Black Man sounds
Good to me.
I would like to give the final touch

Just as he starts to lack faith in that guy in that
Book. That we killed on the cross and came back to life.
I'll hit Black Man with RACISM.
I'll remind him how much people don't like him and
How many people died ofthe color oftheir skin
Then I'll let him know that his cultural Christian
Values are different than the other leaders in the church
I'll also make him believe that the church is segregating
Against blacks and he can't do anything about it
I'll remind him that he had an all white jury in court
And racism is something he can't escape, not even in
His church.
I'll make him get high on drugs in order not to face
His thoughts of destruction.
I'll have him "No Way Out", a place to call home
I'll have his wife leave him and break contact with his family
I'll take away his parole so he can just give up on the
One he used to praise
I'll give him a TV to watch on Sunday mornings
This will keep him in his cell and out of church
I'm the last resort for these other six demons
You might say. I'm the straw that breaks the camel's back.
I'm the head of Satan's tormenting spirits (Uncleanness Depression-
Discouragement-Defeat-Jealousy-Criticism Judgment).
My name is DESTRUCTION.

AMERICA THE HOME OF THE RICH THE LAND OF THE FREE

In 1682 the Indians over powered and captured women and children and adopted them into there tribe.
They would not have brought harm to them, unless they was threatened by the white man
The white man said that the Indians were in human, and treated them as such.

In the 15th century the Spanish arrived
And then came the English and French, and started fighting over land.

The colonial era, in 1780 capture and kid napping selling and trading people, became very Popular.
Europe was alarmed by these attacks
So they brought small pox to the Indians and 70 to 80 Indians at a time, would be found dead From, This deadly disease.

You can be born white or black, But you became a Indian
During the French and Indian war, hundreds were captured, with brutal attacks families were Separated.
For the Europeans the act of being captured by the Indians was a night mere
The captured then went through rituals before being adopted into the Indian tribes

3

After the adoption rituals the Indians would except all races as flesh of their flesh and blood of there blood

The Indians knew how to survive in the wilderness, and they would teach all members in there tribe how to as well.

For the most part the Indians lived with love and peace, with strong feeling for their families

The Indians really valued hunting, and was trust worthy people, they also valued war.

Most of the time in the act of capture it was done in a peaceful was, with a hand shake or one would rest his hand on ones shoulder, to come with them.

The Indians would not rape, and lie, like we have been taught in the movies and history books

The Indians excepted all races who came to them in peace.

Indians got along with the small population of blacks that was here at the time very well

In fact the Indian and black relationship was so strong, they were married and lived together

Some Indians had dark complexions like Africans .

In 1763 the Indians were defeated, and forced to give back there captured

It was a emotional time for all, in fact most of the white people that was captured by the Indians, did not want to go back to living in white society

Some ran away and went back to the Indian tribes, were they was treated with respect and dignity.

Then a short time after Africa was discovered and the violent, savage, ungodly slave trade indorsed by the white man began.

The lying, , raping and separating, the con games, swindling and conniving.

The get rich schemes of increasing the value of your farm, by the blood of the African slave

And the teachings of Willy Lynch bought more pain and suffering on slaves then the pox with the Indians.

Willy lynch will teach slave owners how to brake a slave, they broke horses with more respect

To take the biggest strongest man and tie him to two houses .

 then make all the other slaves watch, as the slave owner beat the horses until they rip the slaves body into two.

Or slowly cut off the private part of a slave so he can scream the more in pain, then stick it in the slaves mouth and kill him.

Shed the blood of children, cut off the heads of babies, and beat and raped women

Just to put fear in the slaves so they will obey.

Then teach the slaves to hate each other, light skin slaves hat dark skin slaves, and teach the slaves, that the most important thing in their lives is to take care of the master.

Willy lynch knew the value of the African slave.

So he made investments in learning about him and experimenting on the slaves
so the white man can live a more comfortable rich productive lives life.

Slavery was one of the best things that could have happened for this country
Slaves were the human computers of yesterday.
Whatever a slave was programmed to do they did, from labor to entertainment.

And in spite of the slave being submissive to their master at all cost
there was still a lot of racial tension and a lot of unlawful activity
Lynching was common, and the only rights that slaves had, was the right to remain silent, and obey.
By this time black communities began to blossom and more black women was getting pregnant
By white men, who never claimed their children or shall I say getting raped.

This was a time of horse and buggy, huts sheds, and out houses, share crops and pig farms
The fields was either full of crops, or empty with a slight gust of wind that after working in the
field from sun up, to sun down, one would look forward to feel that cool breeze
Some days was so hot out in those fields that, some slaves just would faint from the humidity.

We are now in a small town in Virginia
This is a town where most of the slaves that worked locally stayed on the plantation
 to find shelter and what little freedom life had to offer at that point in life.

Tears and shame filled the heart of the common nigger
Some were found hanging in the night fog swinging from tree's.

The law did nothing, and all we did was, asked ' why' 'GOD' Why'
Some got beat with cat and nine tales then salt was put into their wounds to cause more pain.

Most slaves just prayed, they prayed for stuff like, the end of the tribulation
For shoes that fit, and the most common prayer was for the beatings to stop.

And in the mist of all of the turmoil
some even found 'love' one may ask how can someone fall in love at times like this

CHAPTER 2: FREEDOM

THE WORLD IS YOURS

It's important that young black men check
Their history and have a good understanding of self
Who they are, Where they are
How they got here and where they would like to go
Have a good understanding of God
Gods will and self, Gods will for self
If you can crawl, you can walk
If you can walk, you can run
As long as the rivers run
And the earth is by the rain and the sun
As long as the stars shine from the heavens
As long as the rivers run to the sea
You can be whatever you wish to be
You came too far in life and history
Run and faint not
If you want success
All you need to do is
"succeed"
The world is yours.

FREEDOM

It was June 4th 1865 I remember the day as if it was yesterday
After being born into slavery and living that shameful way all of my life
Finally I was told that I was free.

Day say a man by the name of Abraham Lincoln says we be free
Den someone shot and kills him.

Free to take the religion and traditions of the white man
But not go to his church.

Free to celebrate holidays, but not take the day off of work

Free to stay on the plantation but never own land, and give more than half of what crop you grow to the master.

Free to have children but get permission to get married.

Free to leave the plantation but only after you paid your unknown dept to the master.

My family been working on this here plantation since 1789

The first thing I wanted to do was to go find my family in the north .
that's where my pa was from, I would often wonder about him, was he alive, what he look like
do he think bout me.
Here in Virginia I had my great grand ma of whom we called big ma.
I had my grand ma of whom we called madea, and I had my ma which we called Ma Dot.

Dis was all the family I knew, every one elts was sold off, dead, or worked in the big house and
I never had the chance to meet dim.
They call's me Bug eye, for the cause that when I was born my eyes was so big, day looked like
the eyes of a bug.

l downt know how old I am, but im as tall as my ma, and strong as any man on the plantation
Big ma is full of Indian blood, black foot, and im told my pa is African, from Africa
Were we all come from.

My grand ma is Cherokee, I guest I got my dark skin from my pa, being dat my ma is so light
skinned
I worked the tobacco field with my grand ma, She taught me all I know about tabacca
Madea watched over me all of my life, my greatest fear was that one day, one of us would get
sold off and
separated from each other
My master was a fair man, we was glad that he stuck to his word and kept us together as a
family.
Some time latter I understood why.
It was the beginning of a hot and dry summer, we was called to the cotton field for a meeting
with master George.
Master George started off by telling us some stories from the bible
He was acting real funny, I've never seen master open up with us slaves like this before
It was as if he was teaching us to understand this sacred yet forbidden book,
We learn that black mean sin, and white mean holy, clean, and pure.

He say it was Gods will for us to be slaves, and it was a sin to disappoint God
We learn about heaven and hell, he makes me afraid when he tells me about hell

that's a place I don't never want to be, hell be were the devil be, and he is bad
The devil is a evil spirit and he not Gods friend.
Master George say the devil is worst den death
And dats when we heard da news from his mouth, dat wheeze be free, free to come and go as
we wish.
Free to even move, move north, if we want to,
But if we want to be Gods friend we should stay right here on his plantation were we belong
allot of slaves stay because they so afraid to make God angry, and see the devil.

I was born and raised on master George plantation, and dats all I knew
it was during what they called, the American revolution, and Master George was talking about
retiring to a place called mount Vernon
and dats all I, ze knew.

Alls my life I, ze dreamed of being a man who would help my people
To be treated different then now.

To haz my own farm and maybe my own childlens
And I don't think God want me to be, hungry and wiped know more
Besides I, ze want to find my pappy .

So I asked master George if we can leave
He say why you want to leave here ? you got it good here.

We eats when we want to, and we works our own patch of crop
He say I can have a wife and a couple of winches if I wants to

He say if we stay that he will give us our own land
And we can do what we wants to on it
I say we gone, to go north.
He say we can't go north
I say you say we can leave if we wants to.

He say you can't leave until you pay me what you owes me
I sat what we owes you fa?

He say room and board, seed for crop
He names off a bunch of stuff.

I go to my family and tells dem every thing
The next day we just packed up and takes off

So I, ze decided to go north were they say I haze opportunity
And dats what I, ze does, I packed my things and started on my.

Chapter 3: The Death of My Family

REST IN PEACE

A part of me, now gone
And I'm missing you
A part of me, gone to heaven
And I'm missing you
So I sing this song for you
Have a talk with God for me
Live my love in heaven above
Farewell, rest in peace.

A part of me, a part of you
Never apart
Apart of you
Will always be
Here, in my heart
So I sing this song for you
As a prayer to God from me
After all the love from heaven above
Farwell, rest in peace.

Everyone's born to live
Everyone sees it through
Within this world
Of love and hate
We die
Because we do
Everyone's born to live
I wonder when will be my day
I'll live my life and struggle through
I will not go astray.

I'll help to feed the hungry
And brighten up the sad
Do helpful things in life, indeed
For those who never had
It often brings me sorrow
And fills my heart with pain
To see loved ones with crying eyes
Their tears fall like rain
Now that you're gone I'm lonely
Can you see it in my eyes
I see it each and every day
I wonder, I wonder why.

Everyone has to go
Everyone sees it through
Within this world
Of love and hate

We die
Because we do.

After all the love you gave
After all the peace at least
Live happy my love in heaven above
Good bye
Rest in peace
I will see you again my friend
Rest in peace.....

THE DEATH OF MY FAMILY

Big ma, madea and ma dot joined me and dear we was, no horse no buggy just the dings we can carry
We didn't know where we was going, all we knew was to head north so we did
We walked all day until we stumbled into another family headed north.
Dats when we learned that there was some white men riding around killing naggers who was headed north.
So we decided to travel together.

We set up a camp for the night, told some stories and did our best to listen to the strange sounds in the woods, praying not to see know white men, who wants to kill us
Mr. k his wife and their two children, Rose was a baby, and Dreasey was about as tall as I was
Dreasey was short for Edrease
She was a fear skinned well built girl, with short nappy hair, that seemed to bring out her eyes more.

I was in love from the first time I laid eyes on her, she had a strong gentle spirit
She wasn't a women of many words, and as hard as I was trying to get her attention, she was paying me know never mind.

At sun up we started off again on our journey north
About half a days walk, we run across dis small village in the middle of know were, how we found dis place I have know idea, but dear we was.

It was about seven little shacks and a outhouse, all niggras just liven happy and free as could be
Big ma wasn't feeling so well she had a bad fever, so we asked if we can stay for a spell, till she gets better.
Madea was taking care of big ma the best she could, but the fever just wouldn't break
Dats were I learned dat Master George be my pa.

Big ma must have felt death, her head was hot like fire with fever, we was all called into her room for our final good by.
When she made ma dot tell me the truth of who my pa was

It did not hit me at first till about a day or two later, because I was so broke up over big ma not being around know more.

I thought about going back, but what was the use Master George wouldn't treat me know different den he always have because I had nigger blood.

I was so confused at first because I had dreams of what I wanted my pappy to be like, and day wasn't dreams of him being know white master.

Ma dot told me how it was when she first came to the plantation
She told me that day was beating and killing slaves that wouldn't obey, every day
She say Master George and the over seer and sometimes his company, would take little winches and do his business with them all the time.
There was also women taking the men slaves into their rooms at knight
I was to obey or, I was to die.
Ma dot told me how Master George would have her beaten, would sneak in her room at night and how much she wanted me dead, but she just didn't have it in her to kill me, especially after I was born, and she would just look into my big bug eyes and see so much innocents
At that point I really had other feelings about Master George.

After weeks of walking, ferry rides and getting directions from strange folk, dreasey finally opens up to me and we started making conversation.
Once she started talking she just wouldn't stop, and most of the time I couldn't get a word in edge wise.
At night after we camp me and Dreasey would sneak of and do our business
One day me and Mr. k was hunting for something to eat dat night when he asked me
Bug eye do you plane on getting hitched wit my little Drease, or dose you just want to make her belly big?
I was so surprised, I didn't know what to say, so I say, I, ze ant ready to be know pappy .

Dats when he pushed me to the grown and says, youz ant ready to be know pappy, den youz shouldn't be sneaken off wit my little baby know moe.

The next camp night me and dreasey make conversation but she won't sneak off wit me know moe
So I, ze don't ask no moe, and we still walk to make it north.

One night after making camp we settle down to sleep, I had to pee so I walked away to find a tre.
when I hear gun fire and screaming, It sound like medea screaming from the top of her voice
When I runs to see what was going on.

there was white men on horses, dayz beat Mr. k to death, and now dayz burning everything, the camp tent we made, and everything in it was gone.

So I hides until day gone,

When I see baby rose and her ma dead, I, ze get afraid, and I, ze see Dreasey crying I, ze get sad fa her.

Madea was dead too, and ma dot was missing.

Dreasey clothes was torn off of her, and days raped her and left her to die.

I, ze ran to her cry and held her all night we sat there afraid for the white man may come back

The next day I digs graves and says a prayer for da lord to keep dem and to watch over me and dreasey too.

Dreasey was not herself for weeks, she don't say nothing we just walk, and walk.

We don't build camp for two days after the white man left we just sleep outside under trees and walk.

I just got tired and hungry, so eyez stops and hunt food and build new camp wit some of the old stuff I still has from Mr. k .

I wanted to go looking for ma dot, but I was too afraid,

Sometimes slaves would just come up missing, and two maybe three days later they be found.

Some were hanging from a tree, and I was afraid that that's way ize find ma dot, so ize stay

After making camp I took dreasey by the hand to put her in the tent I made wit a old blanket.

To my surprise she won't go in wit me, so we sit outside till sun come back up, she don't say nothing, I do all the talking, I don't have much to talk about but I talk any way

And that's when I made up my mind

If things don't change, im gone take part in making things change.

CHAPTER 4: WHEN I FIND MY FATHER

DO YOU KNOW WHO WE ARE?

Blackman
Who are you?
African American man
Who are you?
Jamaican, African, Ethiopian
No one wants to be an African American
America, America, the land of the rich
The land of the free
We come to this land for opportunity
The melting pot is hot for the African American
Yes, that's what they call me
In this land of opportunity
Some call me nigger, some call me black
Am I home? Is this my land? Where am I at?
Who am I? Whose blood is running through my vain?
How did I get here? Where am I going?
What is my real name?
Black, African American, Negro, Colored
A culture with many names
Do you know who we are?

WHEN I FIND MY FATHER

The next morning we start walking again.
I reach out to hold her hand and she hold me back, I was so happy she hold me back that I hug her and kiss her.
Den she smile and I smile back, dats when I believe we knew dat we still had each other so we walk a little faster.

Dreasey started depending on me like she do her pa
I would take care of her like we jump the broom, I don't mind because I love her.

The next day we run into a old man who say his name is Rabbit, he say they call him Rabbit because he make a lot of babies, I say were all your babies at ?he say he don't know, day been sold off, some die I reckon.
Den he ask us a lot of questions, were yawl going?, were yawl come from, ?who yawl wit?
We tells him everything.
I ask him, how far we from north ? he point and say go dis way two days on horse
I say we got know horse wheeze walking.

He point again and say three night four days dat way, so we walk and we walk, and we walk
A couple miles up the road we see a lot of dust just flying every were.

13

As the dust got closer we see that it was a horse and carriage so we hide in the tall corn on the side of the road.

When the horse and carriage got almost right beside us we see dat its two white men
Yawl niggers come on out, we know yawl in there
Now if we got to go in there and get you, yawl gone get beat.

Dey tell us our names were we bees going and were wheeze come from
Deys tell us everything I'ze tell rabbit
So one gets out of the carriage and the other gets off the horse, and here Deys come headed right for us.
When I sew Dreasey jump out off the bush wit dis short but strong stick
She just started beating and beating dis white man in the head, so when I see that I grabbed the other white man and put my hands around his neck till he don't move no moe.

After me and Dreasey just run as hard and as fast as we could
Den we just falls to the ground out of breath, once she was able to breathe she look at me, and I look at her.
And we just laugh, we laugh until we has know breath know moe
Den we looked at each other again, no laughing no smile
Den we gets up and start walking again.

We come to dis long dirt road, and on the side of the road there was poles, dug in the ground and on each pole there was a man hanging, with feet and hands tied behind there backs.

 some women pop belly and children, and babies, as far as the eye can see niggers hanging
I was looking for rabbit but I don't see him hanging, I wonder if it was dose same white men in the field who done dis, It look like a whole town of niggers, they kills.

We turned into the corn field, we don't take dat way north
Dreasey take her hand from me, and she fall down to the ground and start crying, she say I want to go back we should never leave, please take me back.

I say Dreasey I don't know how to go back, were we go? what we go back to?
We see fields of bodies on our travel north, dead bodies every were
And we pray dat don't happen to us, if we try to go back maybe we be hanging from a tree to.

We see just too much bloodshed, for someone to hold in their memory
So she cried herself to sleep, that's where we lay sleep in the corn field.

When we wake up its still day light so we walk until night fall.

I set up camp and dis time dreasey come in, we hold each other and for the first time in a long time I break down and I cry, I cry for ma dot, madea, big ma Mr. k Dreasey and her ma, I just cried.

Dreasey looked at me like I wasn't suppose to cry, like I was sick or something.
Then she took my hand I looked her in the eyes then I rubbed her soft tender baby face with the back of my hand.
I took her by the back of her neck, i pulled her toward me, as we continued to make constant eye contact.
she took her soft hand and pulled me trousers down, I felt the breeze of the mid day breezed my privet, as I slowly pulled her trouser down, she rubbed my back side and slowly pulled me close to her.
We kissed in a gentle romantic way, then I took my tongue and slowly put it in her mouth, then ran it down the side of her neck, she exhaled, we slowly slide to the ground in unisex.
she laid looking at me as if to say, take me im yours, I laid on top of her and continued to sooth her breast with the tip of my mouth, like I see a man do on the farm, at the plantation. One day I sees them go in the barn and ize follow and watch dem, so I tried to do what day do.

Then she took her hand and put me in her, it was worm soft and tender to me, feeling the warmth of her soft skin against mines, I slowly started to stroke in and out of her with a soulful rhythm, as she gently repeatedly morn in my ear like she was in pain, I would close my eyes and enjoy this wonderful feeling that I never felt before.

For the first time in my life I was making love with deep emotion, I mean we do our business but never like dis before.
we do our business more than once, it was the best time of my life and at that point I knew that she was the women that I wanted to spend the rest of my life with.

I was sad but yet so happy, me and dreasey was in love and as long as we had each other nothing elts mattered, we lost our family and we never had know other company, but we had each other.
Come sun up we walked until we saw anther road, dis one was clean and there was children playing in it.
There was laughter and it seemed as if there was a great since of Peace in the air
I asked one of the children 'witch way north? She say I don't know ask my pa ?
I looked over and laying under a tree was this small old man, with white hair and a long white beard.
We walked over to him and I said my name is bug eye, and dis is dreasey we going north
He looked over his glasses, and with a hard deep voice he said young man 'youz in da north
I was worried about Dreasey cause one more day of seeing death she might loose her mind

I was so happy, dreasey just held me, and the first thing she said was I wish ma and pa was here with us.

that's when I thought about big ma, ma dear and ma dot we started crying but nothing came out of my eyes.

I was happy and sad at the same time.

The old mans name was Earl, we explained to him what we been through, and how we got there.

He invited us to stay with him until we got our self together

Earl was a man of great wisdom, he was a successful business man, who owned his own house and store.

Were we come from that was un heard of, and I must admit I didn't believe him until he showed me the deeds.

Earl gave me a job in his store and taught me how to interact with the white people in the north

Here up north, niggers are still niggers, we are treated better then the way they treat us in the south but we are not equal to the white man, and they let us know it.

Earl also told me that Master George died from a throat infection

So I, ze ask him how he know dat, he say master george was the father of the whole country he was what they call the first president Of the united states.

I don't know what dat mean.

But I did ask myself 'why he let things be the way day is ?

If he be the father of the united states.

Chapter 5: I Took on a New Name

MANUFACTURED AND PRODUCED AS AN AMERICAN

Slayed and betrayed by society
Look into my mind, tell me what you see
Bricks and bars of another penitentiary
Hate a man, enslave a man
And I can't fight it
Looking in the mirror and am undecided
Trying to figure out who the hell I am
Manufactured and produced as an American

The thoughts that I think are of the Bible
The world wants to label me unreliable
I've always got to go the extra mile
Institutionalized for a little while
The agreement that I got is indestructible
You don't fuck with me and I won't fuck with you
I mood swing, like a suicidal dope Fein
I ruff-ruff like a boogie man on Halloween
You think you know me but you still can't understand
Because I'm not your average everyday American

Some may even label me to be a refugee
Some may call me a nigger or a want to be
But until you sat down and read my diary
All you know about me is what you see "g"
I'm not a black man, I'm not an African
Who am I, what am I?
Manufactured and produced as an American
My eyes are on fire, my muscles are tight
My heart is numb
Who am I, Where am I, Where did I come from?

I TOOK ON A NEW NAME

The struggle in the north seems to be more of a political struggle added to the every day struggles of being a nigger.
As long as you don't act to uppity and know your place, and had the understanding that the declaration and the constitution did not apply to us niggers, you can live.

One day I was working in the store when this old whit lady comes in with her servant who happen to have her back turn to me looking through the corn we just put out
I can tell she was a old lady because under her head wrap you can see her gray hair, and the way she moved.
She was old.
Then she turned around and to my surprise it was my ma Dot, 'alive' and well.

17

I was so happy I tried to talk to her, but she smiled and put her finger to her mouth to shush me up.

So we don't say nothing.

They took some corn and left,

I was so happy to see her, I closed the store and ran home and told Dreasey I saw ma Dot.

The next day ma Dot came walking into the store, I knew she was coming back, I just felt it

So I had Dreasey come to work with me that day.

I put the we closed sign up and we hugged and kissed, and just broke down in tears

We was so happy to have each other again.

I tell her all the stories how we got up north, and she tells me that when they took her what they do to her, and how she got away.

How she met this women named Harriet who helped her and a bunch of them get up north

This man named tom help her get that there job as a servant wit room and board.

So I'ze tell her to leave dat dear job and come home wit me.

She say she cant just leave her job, dey might come looking for her and she don't want me to be in danger.

So the next dat I took it apone my self to go talk to the white lady dat she work for

When I got to the house the white lady didn't even let me in, so we sat on the porch and I tells her everything.

How we got separated, and how long we been apart,

The white lady understood and she let ma Dot come live wit me, but she still had to work for her.

Me and Dreasey finally jumped the broom and we are on our second child

We have been living in Massachusetts for two years now, we have our own place, im still working for earl at the store.

The country is still at war for civil rights and I want to take part in it

For some reason I cant forget the people we left in the south.

Im getting word about the way niggers are still being lynched and beaten raped and miss treated.

Earl taught me how to read and right, and I send letters to congress all the time and I never hear back from them, No idea prevails with out the vote of the majority.

I want to take a stand and I know that I cant do it by myself, so I turned to earl to teach me how to organize a committee and get some political help.

The minute I mentioned this to my old friend earl our relationship changed
I went to his house to visit him and his wife would said, he's not home,
And they don't need me at the store know more.

So there I was two children a wife and know job, I don't know how we was to make it
Ma Dot was getting very little money, not enough to live off of her self, let alone feed us to
 With winter time coming and all, All I had was sympathy, empathy and hope.

every day I would go down town to get work, ill get a odd jobs here and there
But for the most part I would watch the white politicians, and I would listen to them and that's
how I learned how white politics worked.
Most time white politicians would talk about working like day goanna get out in them dear
fields and do the work dem salves.

Being self educated made it easy for me to learn the ins and outs of the laws of politics
One thing I didn't learn to fast was more money you had the more say, so, you had, and
most of the time, its not what you know, but who you know, and I didn't have know political
influential people in my life.

One day wile out in the town, I saw a black man standing in the mist of a lot of powerful well
respected white people.
The strange thing was that they treated him as if he belonged, that really caught my attention
So I stuck around until I had the opportunity to approach this well dressed influential man
Once I introduced my self, we hit it off right away.
Even though he hade the political power that I was trying to achieve, he treated me know
different then he treated the white man, he gave me great respect even though politics can be a
dirty game.
After talking politics I explained to him my vision and what I was trying to achieve
He told me that first of all I have to take on a name, know one will elect a man named bug eye
to be there leader.
Then he told me about my dress and my vocabulary my way of speaking, I listened and he
became my teacher.
He taught me that the declaration and the constitution did apply to us, and that we are
people with family and feelings, and due to the fact that we was born in America that we are
Americans.
Americans with the same rights that white folk has, I never had no one speak like this before
So I took in as much knowledge possible, I studied day and night.

Six months has come to pass, and Mr. Douglass introduced me to most of his colleagues and I
began my journey in the political field.

I took on the name Washington because that was the name of my master of whom turned out
to be my pappy
And with that name maybe people would listen to me, and I can make a change.

One day I came home after work and Dreasey was just sitting there on the porch in her favorite
chair, Ma Dot is usually sitting at her side but this time she wasn't.

So I asked Dreasey were ma Dot she say ma Dot never come home from work
So I went to her job and dis time the white lady she work for, let me in.

She took me to the kitchen and ma Dot was sitting in a chair not moving wit her eyes looking
up at the sealing,
I just took my hand and closed her eyes, and we me and the white lady started to cry.

Ma Dot worked for this lady for so long that she loved her like a sister.
We took ma Dot and berried her in the back of my house
I took a bored and I rights on it miss Washington loved by all.

Dreasey took on the job that ma Dot had and we was barely able to make it through the winter
The Irish started coming over from Ireland by large numbers, see there was famine in the land
off Ireland, a big shortage off food

And when they started coming over they started taking niggers jobs
If you had a high complexion your chances of getting work was good, some niggers may even
pass for white
But if they can get a white emigrant to work for them for the same pay of in some cases less
pay, well they chose the white person.

I would meet with Mr. Douglas a lot more and we would talk politics, I learned a lot from
him.
He help me to understand the things that was going on around me
He even had a keen understanding of what the future was going to bring
He said that we will always be the white mans token
And he will always find ways and means to use us to benefit himself.

Chapter 6: I Served My Purpose

WHERE ARE YOU NOW?

Everything has its season, its order
There's nothing new under the sun
A child is born and somebody dies
What is your natural state of mind?
Good and evil?
Everything has its order
As nature takes its course
Life goes on
Who am I to question the universal power
Of its almighty repetitive order
People die because people live
The planet is only so big
So we live, so we die
What is my soul? Do I have a unique spirit?
Is there any reincarnation?
Is there a heavenly waiting place?
Everything has its order
Where did I come from?
Who is good, who is evil?
What is your state of mind?
I'm searching for a reason
Why did you have to die?
Why were you taken away?
Where did you go?
Where are you now?

I SERVED MY PURPOSE

So we became the Washington family from Massachusetts
We met a man who had the same name as my master, his mane was George Washington
The only difference was that he changed his last name to carver
I don't know if we was family, but we talk for a long time
He was a brilliant man, all he really wanted to talk about was peanuts, and what he discover about dem.
Maybe we was kin folk maybe not.
Maybe we be born on the same plantation, maybe not, maybe we got the same pappy.
The plantation was so big, some folk I saw when master george call us to the field, I never see before.

I took my son Daniel with me were ever I went, he was learning as I was learning, our relationship grew and he became a well educated young man.

As I was making my way back to the south, preaching and teaching about Justus and equality

I was faced with great danger, most of the time we escaped death by the skin of our teeth.

I joined up with a man named Vernon Johnson who was brother to Benny Johnson who had a sisters Judy Johnson who was on the same mission as we was on,
They keep talking bout when day die's that they gone have they freedom, and live in dis big house in the sky.

They keep talking bout getting touch with some kind of ghost or spirit, I don't get to close to dem.
Vernon was teaching colored folk how to be more independent, and we became a powerful force.
We would hold meetings in the woods and swamps, some times we would interrupt church meetings with great success to our people.

One night wile setting up camp for sleep we heard a noise in the woods, sound like people running.
So we gets up and looks for were that noise coming from, when we noticed this very dark skinned women.
She was leading about fifteen slaves, day stopped and we met eye to eye a moment of silence and then she say 'we need to come wit her to tom place to find safety Benny Judy and Dot left wit her.
Vernon and I said our good byes and prayed for there safety, that's the last time I saw Judy, and Benny.

Some time in the middle of the night, a gang of white folk on horse back surrounded our camp
Day ask us if we see dis nigger women, we say know, we sees know nigger women
Den day ask us what we doing out there, We say we headed south, and day don't like it because we come from up north
Vernon was a man who spoke his mind and he tells da white man to go on and leave us lone
He say we be free now, and we got rights, So day take us and beat us bad.

Dats when day check our camp and find our paper work
Just knowing we can read and right up set dem
On top of the fact dat we spoke up for civil rights, ment dat we was to die.

So day took Vernon first and hang him high
Then they take me and hang me too
that's when my son Daniel runs off and day don't find him.

Bull whip and beat the slave,
willy lynched in diabolical ways

of weakening the mind
And strengthening the body

We suffer
we feel pain
yet never die

That which doesn't kill me
only makes me stronger

I live through my children
therefore I live
Through generations 'of myself'

God is the power that shapes my way
Therefore my feet are set on a path
That I may follow

CHAPTER 7: TRIP TO BOSTON

REVOLUTION

From the playground to the prison yard
From the basketball court to superior court
From the play gun to the real one
From being a kid to having some
See life goes on by choices
Everyone wants to raise their voices
To give a brother bad advice
Like follow my lead, I got what you need, and this is how to make it in life
So, I used to be a stick up kid
Just to survive that's what I did
Ain't no shame in my game
I produce it and tell it
I can put it on the streets, raise the price and sell it
You know nobody loves me like me
And I love to love my mentality
I used to hang out at the bar room after school
When the only thing we shot was pool
But today we won't go to shoot one another
Wave the peace sign and call each other Brother
It ain't over till the next man die
Take a stand and raise your voice, it's suicide
Some of us are waiting for a revolution
Until then they settle for prostitution
Selling one another short
Lost in this world with no support
Kids killing kids and children making babies
Blame it on the men for what's wrong with the ladies
Life is getting shorter by the bullet
The trigger wasn't made here so why we got to pull it
Liquor stores on every comer
Cocaine, heroin, dust and marijuana
Barbed wire fences, bricks and concrete
A dead end street in a cop town
From the basketball court to superior court
We got no support until we're in the ground
So life goes on by choices
The world wants to shut up our voices
And no one can take a stand
You'll either stay poor and struggle
Or be a dead man
Once in awhile we get sellouts, who forget where they came from
Or even an Uncle Tom who believes he fought the system and won
So I turn into a stick up kid
With all the odds against me, I made a choice, yah I did

I got caught, went to court and got time
And where the hell are all those friends of mine
When you fall home boy, you fall alone
But when you're doing good, people seem to hang to you
Like a gall stone
The systems still making money off me
Like taxes when you work
Jail ain't nothing but a form of slavery
Conditioned to doing time, a slave to drugs, or a slave to crime.

TRIP TO BOSTON

My name is Daniel, the son of bug eye Washington who was a self educated great spokes man
He believed that we as a people have a right to be treated equal.
He believed in racial equality and in civil rights.
I watched the white man hang him on a tree till he die
Yet he not be dead because he lives through me, so I am to carry on his legacy until his dream is fulfilled through me.

Daniel turned out to be a well built handsom intelligent young man
After the death of his father his mother Edrease became so depressed that she committed suicide.
And the last thing he herd about his sister, was that she was struggling and poor
He found himself traveling back to Massachusetts to find his only living relative 'Edrease Washington but he called her by her nick name 'kitty'.

As you know she was named after her mother, and she had her mothers personality
Always loving and caring for others more then her own self.
She was Daniels little sister and he felt as though with ma and pa gone that looking out for her was his responsibility.

Daniel stopped in a city called Boston Mass
Boston had a side of town were only white people hung out, called south Boston a black person wasn't welcome in south Boston day or night, beacon hill and other nice areas like brook line.
the side of town were niggers lived was ran down that was call Roxbury, and some places in Mattapan, or dorchester.
And even if a nigger lived in white folk area, they better not be seen out at night
 most niggers worked in white places like beacon hill for white people who didn't pay much but it was work.

When the sun went down, niggers had to be on there side of town or they may be found dead some were.
Every one was poor and most of the men was coming from or going to the war

I was not interested in fighting or getting enlisted, do to the fact that I didn't really know who or what we was really fighting for.

I mean they say we free but we still hungry poor slaves

And looking for a change

A change that may not ever come, freedom was just an illusion.

I was hoping a train on my way looking for some flower to fry me up dis here chicken I'ze caught.

It took me most of the morning to catch this bird, it was a tuff one, I saw it running wild in the woods.

When I finally got my hands on its neck, I looks up and guest who was standing there looking down on me.

It was this big wide brown man, he say what you doing wit my chicken boy?

First I was afraid thinking It was a white man, thinking I was steeling from his farm

If it was I liken to get my hands cut off, or bull wipped.

But it was Benny, Dot and Judy's brother, Vernon's son, I say Benny dat you, he say how you know my name boy.

He didn't remember me at first because last time he see me I was a little boy.

I say its me Daniel Bug eyes boy, he laugh a little den he gives me the biggest hug, we catch up on old times den he brings me to this big house, he say day works for this good white family

Who gives dem a shack out back to live in wiles day work, as long as day works fa dem dat day can lives here.

So we walks to this small shack a little ways from the house

I see Dot and Judy and we just had a good old time eating and talking about other folks.

Seem like day just want to talk about the lord, and how good he was to them

I tell dem dat pa is dead, and my pa is dead to

And den we gets sad again, and den we started talking about our pappies and started laughing on how day acted, in the old days on the plantation.

I had a good time dat day

I would go visit from time to time until one day ize go back and I don't never see dem know moe.

Ize don't know what could have happened, the shack was a mess, blood every were

I don't know if it was pig, cow, or human blood, cause dayz kill live stock out side

den cut the meat inside I would hate to think dat something bad happened

And it wasn't healthy to ask questions, So all I knows is, dayz just gone.

Chapter 8: I Fell in Love

REMINDED BY A RAINBOW

I've heard many songs
I've read many poems
My sunshine and my storms
This morning was kind of dreary
As I gazed upon the dew
And then I saw a rainbow
That's when I thought of you.

Your eyes are like the stars
As they glitter through the night
Your teeth are like the clouds
So pure and pearly white
Your love reminds me of the sky
So strong, so soft, so blue
And when I see a rainbow
I'll always think: of you.

I FELL IN LOVE

Boston had its Italian communities and its Jewish as well as every one else, but the most ran down degraded community was were the Indians and niggers lived.

Most was ex slaves from the south trying to make a better life for there self up north and Indians that had know other place to go.

The thing that took me at surprise was how foot loose and fancy free people was
They was happy living the shameful way they was living.

When they went shopping at white peoples stores, they had to put the money on the counter and we wasn't able to making eye contact, and say yes sir no sir, and not touch the white mans hand, they take our money, but don't want to touch us.

Most just sat around telling lies, and having fish fries and killing hogs, or doing craft with the Indian people.
I herd a story about this little nigger back down south who was accused of saying something fresh to a white girl in a store.
And some white men found him and beat him to death, they didn't find the body for a long time and when they found the body you couldn't even tell who it was he was beat so bad
Some folks say they beat him because he got fresh with a white girl.

Most niggers didn't even have a change of clothes, the same old sackcloth and hand me downs.

I once saw a white man make a nigger, take the change out of the pocket of a dead nigger, and put, and left the body right there in the street.

Niggers was being miss treated and paying it know attention
When a nigger was missing in the south we go looking fa dem.

We might find dem live, most times we find dem dead, but not here its different
It seemed like the main focus of the day was, what juke joint we was going to jigger at dis weekend.

I remember when we had know time off, weekend or not.
When the sun went down on a Friday night, it seemed like we was on another planet
Niggers drinking and fighting each other, women smoken dat wile weed wit the Indians, like tobacco, running round and yelling like wild hogs.
Niggers steeling from each other, making all kind of babies
Not to many niggers thinking bout schoolin, or teachin
Most niggers dat break the law don't go to jail
Day gets beat half to death, den get sent to the army, or made to work fa who they sleel from.
Dis city life is gonna take some getting used to.

My sister kitty is in a place day call Bridgewater, its about two hours horse ride and I aims to see her.
I settled down in dis Border house for da night and da next day I was on my way
I stopped at dis small farm to feed my mule and get some vittles for my self, when I met miss madam Collins.
Miss Collins lived alone, she say her husband done ran of wit some women who she thought was a friend of hers, but turned out that she was only after her man.

Miss Collins reminded me so much of my ma, she was what I would call a caretaker, her job was to look after the dead.
To be so pretty and full of life I was surprised at her line of work
We hit it off real good so I stayed for dinner and before I knew it a week has gone by, din a month and I just decided to stay and make due
I would work on her farm feeding her live stock and taking care of something's for her.

And for most off the time she did colored folks hair, she can make nigger hair soft and right
And every one from miles around come to her for that
She made dis portion dat she would comb in nigger hair dat made it straight.

She was a good teacher to, she teach niggers how to what she call condition there scalp
They listened and they hair grow fast.
She always help others.
She was a small framed brown skinned women with jet black straight hair, and I loved her personality.

CHAPTER 9: THE BLACK OUT

LORD FIX ME

Now that I'm spiritually free
Now that I'm spiritually free. I once was blind but now I can see
And "finally" I can testify and confess
That the pain and suffering that I was going through
Was just an advantage for my spiritual progress
Hanging with a bad association, I backslide, at a fast pace my life started falling apart
I became broken, misguided, losing the love and integrity of my heart
Entertained by evil spirits, I became a slave to hell
The street life, the drugs, the games, came with slave chains
I became a suicidal dope fiend in a jail cell
Lost, confused, broken and used, "Lord set me free"
I'm filled with grief and disbelief
"Transform my soul and fix me".

---

(1)
"Heavenly Father"
Heavenly Father
Hear
My plea
I give up
I surrender
Jesus
Fix me
(2)
I gave up
On the fight
And I declined
To backslide
Satan got
A hold on me
And I've been unable
To break: free
(3)
I've been hooked
On drugs
And I've been running
The street
Addicted
Afflicted
Alone
And weak
(4)
"Heavenly Father"
Here I am

(6)
Lord I'm living
In a jail cell
Wrestling
With my flesh
Holy Spirit
Overtake me
So if! die
Nevertheless
(7)
"Heavenly Father"
Heavenly Father
It's been a long time
Since I cried
My God
Is "so" good
Yes, he is
"All ofthe time"
(8)
And I cried
Lord, I cried
I can't go on
Without you
I believe
You can change me
I've heard
All about you
(9)
Changing the lives

(11)
Tears ofjoy
Filled my face
The Holy Spirit
Came into the place
My burdens lifted
And I am "free"
yes, Jesus
He fixed me
(12)
"A Holy Holy"
Transformation
It's a spiritual
Awakening
It's a miracle
In "free"
Yes, Jesus
He fixed me.
(13)
"My Lord Fixed Me"
My Lord Fixed Me
Here I am
He fixed me
I was addicted
Depressed, Afflicted
And Jesus
Fixed me.
(14)
"My Lord Fixed Me"
My Lord Fixed Me

In my own jail cell
Doing time
Stressed
Depressed
Suicide
"on my mind"
(5)
Lord fix me
Lord fix me
Her I am
Take my life
I give up
I surrender
Lord knows
I've tried

Of robbers and thieves
Gentiles
and Pharisees
You paid the price
on Calvary
Now Jesus
Fix Me
(10)
"Heavenly Father"
Hear my plea
I give up
I surrender
Lord, Fix me
Here I am
Take my hand
Jesus
Fix Me

I once was blind
Now I can see
Here I am
Born again
Yes, Jesus
He fixed me

THE BLACK OUT

I fell so deep in love with her I forgot about my sister and my mission to help niggers become equal citizens.
I found myself hanging out on Fridays more than I expected to
I would sit around wit the guys drinking fire water or corn shine until I pass out.

It became a daily routine for me
It reached a point, that if I didn't have know fire water or corn shine my skin would crawl and my nerves would shake something bad.

I stopped doing my shores around da farm and miss madam Collins was having my baby, and I just drink more and more, until she just don't want me know more.

I remember her praying for me all the time, would tell her to stop that praying to that mystery God. That slave master God.

If he love us so much den why we going through so much bad stuff
Why looking to heaven, and living in hell
Now don't get me wrong I, ze love the lord, I, ze learn how to read from the bible
But I also know right from wrong, and the way niggers is being treated, well its just wrong.

So Ize drink, ize drink to forget and to feel good
I tried to stop drinking on my own, but it was hard
Sometimes I see things that ant really there.
I sleep on the porch fa most of the day, while she take care of baby jay
One day I just hoped a train and fell asleep.

I passed out on the train and when I wake up I was in Bridgewater
Bridgewater prison for the mentally insane.
When niggers don't act right in this place, they hang him from the walls with chains till he
come to his since, I sew niggers hang from those walls for months at a time, hands and feet
bound
I don't know how I got there, what I dun did, but I was there.

They kept giving me all kinds of medication, and most men there was from da war, day called
dem shell shocked, or on sane
Some of dem just see to much death, and loose dere mind.

Some medication I don't think the doctor knew what they give us, or how they worked
I saw men die just die for know reason, just lay dead, I think it was that medication

Day play wit it, and play wit it, until day find one dat workes
I think they put stuff in the food and drink, to keep us relaxed
Cause I was always sleepy, and drowsy wit know energy.

I was there for six winters before they let me go
While I was locked in that awful place, I did a lot of reading and studying secretly
I became my old self again and now I was going to see my little sister kitty.

And then I was to go back to see Miss Madam Collins and baby jay, who should be about
seven years old now, I think.
I asked the town folk if day knows my sister kitty, not one soul ever heard of her.
I runs into this girl should be about the same age as kitty
She say her name is Eisha 'Beatty', she was from the Stockton family tree, she has a male
friend and a big brother named Natchez Stockton, and a little brother named George Beatty, I
explained to her what kitty look like and she say, you must be talking about Dreasey.

I forgot but I should have known that day don't call her little kitty know moe
Eisha 'Beatty' say yes I, ze knows her, she be my friend, I'll take you to her rights now.

So we walk about two miles across this long field of the most greenest grass you have ever seen.
Then we come up to dis big white house, with 4 big pillars on the biggest porch I have ever
been on.
Eisha Beatty told me, dat the man she was to jump the broom wit come by some times to
check on things.
His name Terry, Terry Brooks, the only black smith in town so everybody knows him
Once I got to know him, turned out to be a friend
I'll go by his shack and help him from time to time, just to keep company.

Eisha was a school teacher, say her and Terry and her two brothers, runs up north to teach, they even build a school house fa niggers.
But white men came and burn it down to the ground, day say niggers ant suppose to learn certain stuff.
My ma teach me if they don't treat you right, don't expect dem to teach you right.

I believe Eisha cause dats what kind of folk my sister like to keep company wit
She was a soft spoken short dark completed lady, seem to have good since.
So I asked Eisha 'Beatty' is dis Dreasey house?
She say know, dis house belong to a Madam CJ Collins, Dreasey live here until Miss Collins husband come home, Day say he loose his mind or something happened

Me, I don't think he commen back, day been waiting for years now
Miss Collins, she a well off nigger, day say she make her money making oil, they call conditioner for nigger hair dat make nigger hair soft and right, like white folks.
When I walked into this big house it looked like nothing I ant never seen before
And coming down the stairs was this young man who look like me, and I say to him, is you baby jay?
He say sounding like educated white folk speaking proper English,

they don't call me baby jay know more, my name is Daniel, Daniel Washington
I thought he would be about six or seven years old, turned out the boy was sixteen.
I said my goodness where did all of the time go
And standing at the top of the steps was the most beautiful women I have ever seen
She looked so clean and pure and natural.
She said very loudly, the time went into that jug of fire water you was holding on to for so long
And we laughed, then she came down stairs and gave me the biggest hug I ever had, then we cried, and I was back with my women again

And dats when I saw my sister

CHAPTER 10: K-K-K KILLING

THE RIGHT TO REMAIN SILENT

A constitutional democracy, a way we'll never win
The north was singing when the saints go marching in
The south was singing Dixieland
Lincoln was singing the national anthem
And the Declaration of Independence
Was for what we all wanted: rights
Frederic Douglas was a great spokesman
Who worked with the underground railroad
With people like Harriet Tubman
Some slaves left the south looking for
The promised land, traveling days and nights
For what we all wanted
Rights
There's a new form of slavery
Prison, the long and lonely ride
Where some are victims of circumstances
But most are victims of genocide
I'm told I have high blood pressure
And high esteem, so they call me violent
With that they give me one right
The right to remain silent
Some speak with expressions
A frown with eyes of pride
But I speak out in writing
So I write in silence
My struggle in genocide.
Dark was always wicked
So I aim to see the light
After being told I was wrong for so long
I wonder, what's it like to be right?
Was Vernon Johnson right, by striking back?
Was Martin Luther King right, by being for peace and not attack?
We're the pilgrims, right? By transporting slaves
Was it right to kill a father
And make his children dig his grave
Is it right to kill nations, African and Indian tribes?
Either die or get drunk off the gin you used for bribes.
But I have the right to remain silent
What I say or do can be used against me in the court of law
I have the right to an attorney
If! can't afford one
You will appoint me one, from the court of law
Yah, right!
    You just want me to remain
        "silent"
    I GOT MY RIGHTS

K-K-K KILLING

She was so small the last time I laid eyes on her, and now she is a grown women
The first thing she say to me is, don't come over here with all that little kitty stuff as you can
see I ant little, and they don't call me kitty around dease here parts.

So I say what do you suppose I call you den?
She say I go by my middle name now Christine, but everyone calls me Tina.

So we sit and talk for a long time, and the next day we sit and talk some more
We up north now, we got money and the only thing we don't do is get married.

So I ask miss Collins to be my wife, she say yes and that made me very happy
Looking into the eyes of my son, he didn't seem to be so happy
It was funny how he act, he act like he was too good to be my son.

So I sat him down and I told him about my pappy
And what my pappy told me about his pa, his grand ma
Were we come from, how we got here, what the worlds like, and what we doing today.
How many of us was shot down in cold blood, hung from trees
So we can live today.
And we don't even know their names.

How niggers hung from trees praying
From pregnant women to preachers and children
How they still burn churches in the south, and some still in slaved
Getting raped and robbed from who day really is
We talked for a long time, until he just broke down in tears and he say daddy were you been all
this time?

Two years gone pass now and we moved back to the south for a spell, so I can continue my
work as a actives 'looking for a change' To help my people.

We in a place called Indianapolis now
My wife still doing hair and ize is ducking from a group of white folk called the klu Klux klan
The k-k-k is a group of white folk who is killing niggers for trying to have what they got.

Day say, day Gods chosen true red blooded Americans
 day was called white supremacists
day wanted to stop niggers from living in America, or living at all
Day don't want us to have nothing
Not even the right to vote and a right to go to school and learn.

One day I was out in the field teaching a group of niggers about equal rights and how we can end the segregation against niggers.

When theses two white men approached me and they said that they don't take to likely to my kind.

They given me till sundown to move or bad things is gonna happen to me and my family

No one has the right to tell me that I can't talk to my people its call freedom of speech it's in the constitution I said.

One of the men said with a voice of hate, you've been warned nigger

With my son by my side I just ignored him and kept on teaching .

That night when we settling down for bed, I herd gun fire

And then the windows on our house was broke.

Then they started burning the horse barn down, so I ran outside to try and scare them off with my shot gun.

When they surrounded me, then they got off of their horses

One of them grabbed me, the other put a rope around my head.

Somehow I got out of the rope and began to run to my family

Then I heard a gun go off, I didn't feel nothing at first, but I couldn't move my legs

So I just lay there with my sister wife and child looking on

The horse men then road off.

So I sits there with my folks standing over me, and we just watched the horse barn burn to the ground.

The next morning they started to pack what they can find

My wife had some money buried under the house, so she dug that up.

My son picked me up and put me on a wagon, they took the bullet out my back, patched me up the best they can, I still couldn't feel my legs, I was crying out 'I can't feel my legs' I can't feel my legs'.

I just felt so helpless, I don't want to die, not like this

On the way to the train station that's what I did ' I died.

> *bull whip and beat a slave*
> *Willy lynched in diabolical ways*
>
> *Of weakening the mind*
> *And strengthening the body*
>
> *We suffer,*
> *we feel pain*

Yet never die

That which doesn't kill me
Only makes me stronger

I live through my children
Therefore I live through generations of myself

God is the power that shapes my way
Therefore my feet are set on a path
That I may follow

CHAPTER 11: TRIP TO AFRICA

EXPECTING DIFFERENT RESULTS

On my journey miss directed
Having everything under control and neglected
Friends and Foes and those I don't know
Accepted and Rejected
Now I stand alone ... feeling the pain.
Friends and Foes can't remember my name.
Who got it good, is my sad song
Lonely only because my goods are gone
On my journey miss directed... used and confused
I lost the game once again.
Having everything under control, I set out to win but I lost again.
I can only blame myself and no one else
Doing the same thing over and over again...
Expecting Different Results...

TRIP TO AFRICA

From 1914 to 1918 the whole world was at war
Germany was stopped from enslaving Europe
The u-s-a still had enslavement
 it was the law.
Two hundred dollars, for a child and even less for a male adult.
But a nigger winch, she was the prime of the stock
Day bids fa her, and the highest bidder, got himself a bed wormer, a cook, a maid,
And someone to bear more suckling all in one.
June 4th 1865 we was suppose to be free
After the war most niggers left the plantations, in some cases all the slaves left
a lot of white slave owners was so conditioned to having slaves, that they couldn't do for their selves.
Some women was left alone after their husbands died in the war, they did not know how to survive on their own, so a lot of them committed suicide, when others became so close to the slaves that stayed.
When they died they left the slave the deed for ownership to their houses
Some niggers owned land and kept it in good shape.
They raised their children, and their children's, children on that same land
In some cases the white man found out and took the house and land from them by using the law.
And niggers had no education about most laws, so they didn't know all they knew was to move or die.

My dad came into my life and left as fast as he came

In the short time we spent together, I did get to know what kind of man he was
And what kind of a man he wanted me to be.

My ma wanted me to have an education, My dad wanted me to have self respect
He told me even if the world don't respect me
I must learn to respect myself and as long as I respect myself
The world would one day respect me, 'I am a man'

And one day things gone change
With the knowledge that he gave to me
And the wisdom that he molded into my heart
as long as I carry his name
I to will carry the message of freedom and democracy.

I am to take this message to levels that my forefathers was un able to
I can because they was poor, and I'm not.

They didn't have no education, and I do
They lived in another time, another error
I believe that we stand a chance today.
For a short time the focus wasn't on niggers in such a aggressive way
Do to the fact that there was some German man setting up and killing Jewish people.

They say he had Europe, but was also fighting for Russia
They say he put some Jewish people in slavery, dat he done killed most of dem.

My aunt Tina and my ma wasn't too happy about the decision I made to follow my dad's
footsteps.
I remember clearly the day that I left home, how they begged me to stay
But there was something greater then I was setting me on a mission, and moving my spirit
To go on a mission to go back to where it all began 'Africa'

I had all of my legal papers in hand, and there I was on a plane for the first time
It was good to get away.

CHAPTER 12: TRIP BACK TO THE STATES

WHY TALK ABOUT ME?

People talk about me
Because I got big lips
But I like who I am
Most black people got big lips
And I'm a black man
People talk about me
My hair is nappy
Nappy like hair of a lamb
That's the way I was born
And I like who I am
People talk about me
My skin is dark like coal
Like oil, like the rich dark earth
I've been this way since birth
And I like who I am
People talk about me
I look into the mirror
And my father I see
And some say my children
Also look like me
I love my family
And I like who I am.
So why would I want to be
Someone other than me
When "I" like who "I am"
Why talk about me?
When you talk about me
You talk about everyone on my family tree
Do yourself a favor
"Check your own history"
Look into the mirror
All of the dirt "you have done"
Then ask yourself
Am I God's son?
Generations down
Your goal in life
Was to make my life hard
And you don't even realize
That "I'm the child of God"

TRIP BACK TO THE STATES

When I arrived I felt so far away from home, due to the fact that I wasn't just a nigger
But I was an American nigger, and that was worst.
Africa was very different in its social standards

Racism was still at its high point, the sharking thing was that niggers was racist against each other.

Some niggers, even sell niggers, to the white man fa small things, like looking glass, or fire water

It was a real surprise to me when I saw my very first African slave master

Slavery wasn't as popular as it was in the states, but it was strong, all the same

They enslaved each other just because they was from different tribes, and worshiped different Gods.

the Ashanti tribe didn't like the Bakongo tribe, the Bemba tribe was racist against the Amhara tribe and so, on,

I stayed in a little village outside of Kenya, were we would hunt for our own food and cook it without some saying we steel of their land.

There was many different languages and tribes, and many different rules fa living

 some was at peace with each other, and some at war.

After being there for a year or so, I was able to tell one tribe from the other

Mostly by the look on their faces when they saw me.

some gave me a look of hate that you wouldn't believe

I stayed in constant contact with my aunt and my ma.

I also met a young lady, her name was cabbala which meant 'thinking 'in her language

She was having my suckling and we was in love.

I knew one day I would have to leave, and I would have to decide if they was coming back to the states with me, or shall I leave them there.

I started to teach the people about unity and equality, reading writing and math

some didn't like it one bit.

My life was threatened several times, They even burn my house down

And that's when I decided to take my Cabbala with me.

In fact Africa is much like the states, racism still exist strongly

The only difference that I can see between me and the Africans is, that they at least, know who their family is, and most importantly 'they know who they is, and were they come from.

I have no place that I am welcomed enough to call ' home' were is my home?

And I don't know what tribe I come from, no matter where I go.

So I took my Cabbala and headed back to the states

Before we left cabbala wanted to stop, and say good bye to some of her family in a village where they was called the Culu tribe.

These niggers were true African worriers, they communicated to the beat of the drum, just like the Mandingo worriers that I met in the states.

to my surprise the Mandingo worriers was at war with the Culu tribe.

most slaves used the same drum to communicate in travel, like what we called the underground rail road.

I was able to see the things that we inherited from our ancestors

But here in Africa they treated me different then the people that was born here, they say that I had white blood, therefore for the most part I was a outcaste from some rituals, my blood was poisoned with white blood, and the Culu tribe did not allow me to take part in there rituals of song and dance to their ancestors that died and in communication with their God.

That night I just sat by the hut, watching the flames of fire, while Cabbalas family gave her a farewell festival, at sun up we got our legal papers and went on our way.

Finally we made it back to the states, there I was a sack full of clothes in my hand just arriving at the train station.
Trying to make it to my ma, ma and my sister Tina who was still in Bridgewater mass, in the big house waiting on my arrival.
I was not paying it any attention, but my wife was still dressed with her regular African clothes
They may have been excepted in Africa because that's how they dressed.

But here in the states, she looked like a pregnant house nigger
That was the worst train ride in my life, because that's how white folk was treating her
And I didn't like it one bit, she wasn't know pregnant house nigger.

Once we sat down on the train white folk was just staring at her, with ugly looks
But it was another nigger who opened her mouth first, why we always putting each other down.

She say real ignorant like, ''don't you know dat we ain't slaves know Moe?
What masta got you knocked up?, and what plantation you come from niggers?
niggers started to laughs and make jokes about my wife.
My wife said, I is never know slave, and what's this house nigger?, you call me
then I got upset and I told them people.

My wife is from Africa, were we all comes from before we bought here
We bought here by boats, sick and some dead and don't make it
All of us not born here, some us from Africa.

in Africa it is a custom with her tribe to dress this way
Slaves dress like Africans, not African like slaves.
My ma and her ma dress this way, they inherit this dress from our ancestors in Africa
The difference between a American nigger and a African nigger, is dayz from Africa
And dayz know where day from.

I was preaching and teaching about how things can change, and I had every ones attention
Niggers started asking me questions and I was giving them good advice.

I wanted to start my own campaign for better education and equal right for niggers
But I was not alone, and I knew the dangers that may come with that, and I didn't want to put my wife and unborn suckling in any danger, so then I shut my mouth and we get off of the train.

"Protect you queen"
My blood was so hot, when we made it to ma Collins house, I didn't even here when Tina tell me that ma walker was sick in bed.
By the time I realize what she say I ran to ma walkers bed side, and there I was for most of the night.
When sun come up Cabala yelled my "water break the baby coming"
So I runs to ma Collins room to get her, so she can pull the baby out, when she don't move
I yells for Tina to come look after her, when Tina tells me that ma Collins dead.

I was so confused that I forgot all about Cabbala giving suckling
When I come to my good since Tina was already in the room with rags and water
She closed the door and tells me to leave.
I don't leave I just stay at the door for a long time, just thinking about ma Collins, and all the good times we have together.

When my suckling born, I hold him in my arms and I name him C-J after Miss Collins middle name.
C-J Washington
The news traveled fast that miss Collins dead, and people come from all over to view her body and say good by.
We dug a hole in the yard and lay her in it, with a board I made and on it I rights
"Miss Collins mother of Daniel Jr, wife of Daniel sir, big ma of C-J Washington sleep in peace"
Sometime I sit and talk with her like she still alive.

We live at ma Collins house for about 15years before my sister little took sick with the pox and die.
We dug a hole and put her next to ma Collins
Cabala left me a short while after that, and went back to Africa.

Me and C-j Didn't have enough money or help to run the house and farm so we sell, and we packed and headed back south.
We made it as far as to Chicago, and settle down
I started a small farm of cotton and tobacco, I gave C j my teaching books and he was steady learning.
One day I was working in the field and just collapse
I guess I got to old, and that's where I die, right there in the field.

Bull whip and beat a slave
Willy lynched in diabolical ways
of weakening the mind
And strengthening the body
We suffer we feel pain
Yet never die
That which doesn't kill me
Only make me stronger
I live through my children
Therefore I live through generations of myself
God is the power that shapes my way
And my feet are set on a path that I may follow

CHAPTER 13: MISSING IN ACTION

The name of this poem is "ME"
I am "ME"
And proud to be "ME", "A Black Man"

ME

"I'M" the first man
"I'M" in the image of my creator
I'M" a descent of kings so I stand as King
"I'M" a B.B.King so I entertain as a King
"I'M" a Rodney King, A Don King, so I conquer as a King
"I'M" a Martin Luther King so I preach as a King
"I'M" a King David, A Solomon, so I rule as a King
I am Me

So why would I want to perm my hair 'straight'?
So why would I want contacts just to change the color of my eyes?
That's not being me, "I'M ME" just as I am
A descendent of kings, "The king of all kings"
The image of my creator
And the greatest creation of them all, it's "ME"
"I am me"
Lamb hair, hair like wool, big eyes, big lips, big shoulders, big legs
Strong arms and a strong back
"I'm me", I'm "black" created exactly in the image ofmy creator
I AM ME

There's style in my walk
The way I strut with rhythm
There's style in my talk
The way I strut with rhythm
Fashion designs have been made
By the way I style my clothes
And the way I strut with rhythm
It's a heavenly song I dance to
"Proud" to be "Me"
The way I strut with rhythm
So why would I want to be anyone other than "ME"?
When I am what I am - why?
Since I have been created
The enemy has invaded
Trying to kill my seed forever for sure
Because my seed is so holy, so blessed and so pure
Why am I such a threat?
To the international known beast
After all I've been created in the image of love
In the image of peace, generation after generation
Killing after killing, it's been a conspiracy
Why? Because I am what I am, and always will be.

A black man
And proud to be
"ME"

MISSING IN ACTION

I am C J Washington son of C J Washington sir
I live in Chicago with my wife
 she from a place called Kansas
Who so happens to be a white woman.

That should let you know how much times have changed over the years
The year is 1960 and I am native born out of Africa
Now living in America with my wife.
Times are so hard for us, with her being white and me being African
Negroes have no rights.
The only right we have, is to wash the white man's floor and raise his children
Be his servant and get pain peanuts.
The world is a toilet bowl, and we get treated like the mess in it.

A man named Malcolm X is running around preaching and trying to teach Negros to live
right
He was a man that went to prison and changed his life, now he trying to help Negroes
Eat, dress, and live better.

 Say the white man is the devil and they don't like that
He say in the white man's dictionary, niggers is called a black person a second class citizens
After all we did building this here country.
They gone call us second class niggers
Come to find out the word nigger really mean a ignorant person.
The difference between a Negro and a nigger is, a nigger don't no know better.

But in the Webster's encyclopedia dictionary it said a nigger is a black person of know social
standards.
Second class citizens
Second class, the foundation of this country was built on our backs, death and suffering.

A lady by the name of miss Parks messed around and got thrown in jail for sitting on the front
of the bus.
Mr. Rev. King helped with a boycott and people was walking to work
No one took a bus, until they was in agreement with Negroes to let them sit were they wanted
to on the bus, and it worked, and once again those that worked at white people's houses, raisin
their children and scrubbing there floors was on time for work, and wasn't tied once they got
there.

That same preacher rev Martin Luther King Jr is trying to get equal right for us
he lead a march in Washington and gave a powerful speech called, I have a dream, it made a
big difference, a big difference but not big enough.
Some whites joined blacks and protest equal rights for blacks, they got beat too, some almost
got beat to death, they travel cross country on a bus, they call themselves freedom riders.

The liberation for equal rights for women rights was won, and Negroes are still and have been
fighting for equal rights, all there life, for generations.

Hate was still in the hearts of many, or shall I say fear
When we went to restaurants, even fast food, we hade to go to the back of the building to get
served.
We paid the same price as white folk, they took our money but wouldn't let us in to dine, with
them, Because we were Negro.
You learn how to play the game quick, when it came down to how to act in front of the white
man.
We say, yes sir no sir, to make him happy.
We cook, we clean, we play dumb and act stupid.
But when we get alone we told some jokes about them funny acting people
And how we fool then into believing that we don't know no better.

The K-K-K is still putting on white sheets, and burning crosses in Negros front yards
They hide their faces, but for the most times we know who do what.

White police men and fire men is killing people, even woman and children
When Negros try to protest for equality.
 The government, from the mayor, on up to the president is racist.

They come with the water hose and dogs
The water feel like you being stoned, like in bible days
And they make them dogs bite any Negro standing.

And a group of white people call their self hippies, running around high off of T-H-C, and
L-S-D and all other drugs they can get their hands on.
The government, from the mayor, on up to the president is racist.

The police are looking for a man named Charles Manson, they say he been killing white people, whole
families at one time, and had a lot of help to, Some of those who help him worship him like he
a God.

The black panther party is using strategy, to beat the white man, at his own game

47

by using his own laws against him
The black panther party is a progressive political organization that stood in the vanguard of the most powerful movement for social change.

And while the white man fighting and killing Negros, the country is at war with Vietnam
And it seems that president Kennedy is more focus on that war
then the war right in his own back yard.

I found out later on that it wasn't true
That Kennedy was really trying to help Negroes, but he couldn't help us all by him self.
I also found out that there was allot of lies in the history books
And we wasn't being taught the truth about allot of things.

Things was just getting to out of hand around these here parts
It was a war that I couldn't win.
So I made a choice to take my wife and mother and move to Hawaii
Fare away from this mess.
I been to Hawaii wile in the military and I liked it so much that I said one day I would like to move there so I did.

 poem ; a special day your first day on earth
My shadow my son

The year is 1961 we just had our first son
I name him Barack, it is a African name which means 'chosen one'
There is some racism here but not like I had experienced in the south.
I went into the military at a young age
I was influenced by my father who served in the Patton's army
And my mother was the manager at a bank.

So I had a good education, and my goal in life was to give my son one as well.
We was living well until I was called for duty to go fight for my country
after Martin and Malcolm was shot down in cold blood
I was ready to do something.
But not for a country that really didn't care to much about me
but for my children and their children, so I went.

My wife didn't want me to go, because so many people was going and coming back home dead, or not coming back at all.

The government didn't fulfill all of their promises and allot of woman and children was left fatherless and poor.
I went because I believed in change, and I wanted things to change so bad, that I would have laid down my life' to make a difference for the next generation
And that's what I did, I died, and never returned home again
"always protect your queen"

Bull whip and beat a slave
Willy lynched in diabolical ways
Of weakening the mind
And strengthening the body
We suffer we feel pain
Yet never die
That which doesn't kill me
Only makes me stronger
I live through my children
Therefore I live
Through generations of myself
God is the power that shapes my way
There for my feet are set on a path
That 'I' may follow

CHAPTER 14: CHANGE WE CAN

GOD REUNITE ME AND MY SON

Dear Son
How can I explain to you why I could not be there?
I know you've had your hopes and dreams
Your cries and your prayers
I could start by expressing
How life is so unfair
The prisons, the drugs, the crimes, the racism
And people who just don't care
How I tried to hold onto you from behind these
Prison walls
With bitter stressful feelings, relationships and
Collect phone calls
How I reached out to your Mother
As she moved on in silence
How I cried to the parole board
But my record had too my violence
The plans I had for you and I since you were a little kid
But Daddy made mistakes
And Daddy caught a bid
I know you've heard a lot of things and you've
Tried to understand
Maybe you won't until you experience life's struggles
When you become a man
I've played the hand life dealt to me
I did my best with the hand I had
I will always love you son
Sincerely, Your Dad
There's a bond between a father and his son
That could never be broken
Like Abraham and Isaac
A bond since the word of God was spoken
So no matter what happens in life
Whether they love us
Whether they hate us
You are a special part of me
And no one can separate us
I wanted to be there with you
On Christmas and your birthday
But I have to wait for my release date
And for God to make a way
I wished to be with you
And do the things you like
To teach you how to skateboard
Play ball and ride a bike
I've made bad choices son
And with that I had to pay

And God willing, I'll have the chance
To make it up one day
I pray you don't hate me
For the wrong that I've done
Try to stay strong
It won't be long
For God to reunite me and my son.

CHANGE WE CAN

My name is Barack h Washington
The son of C-J Washington
I was born In Hawaii in august 4 1961
I am being raised by mother who is a white lady from Kansas
My grandmother who is from a place called Kenya in Africa
And also my grandfather.

The year is 1977
I am sixteen years of age and I just graduated high school
I am struggling to get scholarships and a student loans to go to college
Do to the fact that I am colored.

Why? Well most colored people was just pushed through school
I know people who, graduated and still can't read.
And those who have gotten student loans, failed and was unable to pay them back
I am what you may want to call middle class.

Do to the fact that we live in a good neighborhood
But my family are hard workers, and we are still struggle
I wasn't excepted, to hang out with white boys, even though we lived in the same community.

So I would hang with those of my own race
For the most part all we did was play basket ball, and chase girls.

My mother wanted to get me off of the streets fast, she was afraid that I would end up dead or in jail.
All I wanted to do at that point was fluff my fro, and flash my bell bottom pants, with my plat form shoes, all they ever heard me say was right on brother or sister, or I can dig it, power to the people, or something.

So she got together with my grand ma, and they got me a scholarship
I went to college and remained focus on my studies, and had a lot of success.

I made the basket ball team, and became a very popular young man in my interest in politics
And while I was getting my education the world took many changes.
From music changing from rock and roll to rhythm and blues, heavy metal and hard rock, funk and now this new music called gangster rap.

At first it was young brothers expressing themselves, by the life style they was force to live in to young brothers shooting and killing each other by high numbers.

to silence the violence one million men marched in Washington
Alex Haley wrote a book called roots which opened the eyes and hearts of millions
To understand where we came from and how we got here
It made a difference, but not a lot changed.

The ghetto life turned into one big front off gold chains, big earrings, and drug sales
If a black person wasn't dyeing from drug overdose it was by the hands of another brother
The system then took on a new strategy, the new form of slavery was jail time.

The government would pay the state 40 thousand a year for housing inmates
So laws changed and sentences got strict

Most of the inmates doing time was young black men from the inner city
A man by the name of rev j Jackson, a well known minister, who started a coalition
He took a stand to pave the way and run for president, he didn't even get nominated
All of the gifts that I inherited kicked in, and once I graduated college my dream was to take that same road, and run for office.

Then the biggest night mere that could have ever happened did
t-h-c l-s-d opium, black beauties, orange sunshine, pink heats, red weed, and tie stick, and dope addicts was once our biggest drug problems.

Liquor stores was and still is on every corner in black communities
That was nothing compared to CRACK COCAIN, when crack cocaine hit the streets in the urban communities, it instantly filled the cells in the prison system.
Less rehabs and more prisons was being built, as crime increased dramatically
The ripple effect was, that we could not borrow bread and sugar off of each other because we didn't trust each other know more.
There was more homeless people, and some even got paid for snitching
Even the prison system changed, from convicts to inmates
It was a strategic was of politics and crime lords, making millions off of the system
We are knocked down but not knocked out.

Chapter 15: Karma

WHAT COMES AROUND, GOES AROUND

We have reached a point in society were the economy has affected us all
There are home owners who have been forced to foreclose their homes.

Unable to sell them because the housing market is upside down
Unemployment is at a all time high, it hasn't been this bad since the depression, and with the deficits the country is billions of dollars in dept.

Roaches and rats fill the homes In the inner cities
Prostitution, aids, and Drugs have infected the neighborhoods in the inner city.
From young rich white people to poor young black people have become addicted to dope
Or crack cocaine, it is an epidemic and we all feel the pain.

One of the only time the two races unite, in the inner city is when white people come to town to buy drugs
Most of the time when a white person comes to the gutter to get drugs, they end up getting ripped off, or robed.
And if you come to a certain neighborhood after dark you can come up missing
Young black people rule the street corners, apartment hallways and back alley ways.

The same treatment black people once got when interring the white community is given back
The police come in multi colors, and very few can be trusted.
When the black man is faced with injustice today they riot, even have the right to take people to court.
A man by the name of Rodney king was beat with the Billy clubs of several white police officers.
As he pleaded for his life in agony, and the only word he was able to get out of his mouth was, and I quote, 'Cant we all just get along"

The black community, went in a uproar and rioted, violence begot violence, black people started to demand equal rights, It was a sign of the time

A well known black actor and retired football player by the name of OJ Simpson was accused of murdering his white wife.
The black community had his back so strong, just for the fear of another race riot, he was found not guilty.
When he was released from jail, he gave no props, to the black people that stood behind him during his trial.

In 1989 a black man was accused of stabbing and killing a pregnant white women
The police men ran through the mission hill projects of Boston mass, arresting black people and throwing them in jail at will.
Kicking in doors and violating the right of the people
They arrested a man named Willie Bennett, a black man and accused him of the crime.
Come to find out her boy friend, a white man, the father of the baby, killed her, the police didn't suspect him until he killed his self.
A white lady took her little children and put them in her car and rolled them in a river and they drowned.
The first thing that came out her mouth was a black man did it
The black community was being shook down, and once again black people was getting locked up and beat down at will.

These are just a few cases of the in Justus that is happening in the communities in America, every day.
There are more white people going to jail today then ten years ago, the only difference is that black people are getting more time for the same crimes.

When you're in the fox hole and fighting a war, it don't matter what color the person is fighting beside you
What matters is that you are fighting for each other, and able to save each other's life
Some from the opposite race have even became brothers in times of war.

Some of the white race wants equal opportunity, right alongside the black race today
But If you was black and crossing the street, walking towards a white persons car you will hear a click, click, noise, that is the doors being locked.

If you wasn't working in the black community or buying drugs, you must be a cop or a detective, or you didn't have no business in the black community.
 And if a white persons car broke down on the wrong side of town, they was so afraid
That they will leave the car and everything in it to try to get out of that side of town.

There was once a time when black people couldn't go into the white neighborhood, and now the white people are afraid to go into the black neighborhood
And this is America, the land of the rich and the home of the free.

THE HUMAN TOUCH

You can fight my wars, get right up there, on the front line
But don't touch me
I'll watch you play basketball
But don't you touch me

I'll watch you play football
But don't you touch me
I'll cheer you on, you can be my favorite player
But don't you touch me
I'll watch you fight, even call you champ, my champ, the people's champ
But don't you touch me
I'll eat your cooking, teach me how to cook that good old soul food
But don't you touch me
We can talk but you have to agree with me, don't you be too aggressive
We can look at each other, not too much eye contact, I'll listen to your music
But don't you touch me
Clean my house, wash my car, teach me how to dance
Shop at my store, give your money
But don't you ever touch me, without my consent
OK, I'll shake your hand, you have done a good job
But that's it, only a handshake
Don't pat me on the back, don't come around me after dark
You and your kind stay away, or I'll call the police, you understand
Stay away, don't move into my neighborhood, and most of all, don't you touch me
"News Flash" "News Flash" "Today's top story"
A young white male was struck by a car tonight
He lost a lot of blood and needed a blood transfusion
The hospitals only Afro-American doctor performed
An outstanding open heart operation
When the young white man awakened
He also agreed to the doctors professional performance
As the young white male sat there
With tears in his eyes
Not knowing that the blood donor was also black
....the black man's blood saved his life
Told the doctor that he had done a fine job
The doctor then said, "1 could not have done it by myself'
"You also have a strong will to live"
The white male slowly put his head down
With a little smile on his face
And with a small gentle heart, he then said,
"THANK YOU, I'M TOUCHED"

In spite of all the difficulty we face today, black people have major trust issues with each other
All other races can stick together and support each other.
Most other families can go into businesses with each other, and have success right in the black community.
Their children are driving nice car got money in the bank and using credit cards
While most black children are fighting for their life in court, they are on public aid
And bailey have enough money for a bus pass
people watch the common young black man as if he is going to rob them or kill them.

FLICK THE SWITCH, THE POWER IS ON

INTRODUCTION

There are too many obstacles that keep us divided
And it's sad to even say
That to many of us are brainwashed, rocked to sleep and too blind to see
The things that keep us mentally, spiritually and socially divided
We can band together at times when the going is good
We can stand together at times when we think we're safe
But when the fireman starts to spray us with the water hose
Or the dog trainer puts the K-9 on us
It's every man for himself
Someone once told me that that's what it's all about
"it's all about self'
While we all suffer, our mothers and children suffer
Because of this division
Divided and left standing alone
And here we are, so quick to fight each other
Over small matters that can easily be resolved
Over things like a basketball game
"it's my turn on the telephone" and etc
Calling each other out of there name
"man don't disrespect me"
While we are being disrespected in other areas every single day
In many different ways
But our focus is on the wrong issues
And it's blinding
Too blind to see, why our family got to pay so much for
That phone call? For that TV?
What's all of this supply and demand jumping off about
Like crabs in a barrel constantly pulling each other down
Back biting and screaming with jealousy and strife
Misjudging and prejudging each other in negative ways
Judging each other by the style of sneakers we wear
Judging each other by the way we braid or cut our hair
Judging each other by how much canteen we get
Who got what and what's he doing time for
Instead of putting each other down
Let's start pulling each other up
By being persistent to assist each other
Do you have any sneakers? If not, how can I help you get some?
Let's go to the library and work on our cases together
Let's figure out some way we can get out of this mess "together"
Let's stop living in darkness
Flick the switch, unite and turn on some power
So we can all get a grasp of things
So we can all see the light
So our families won't be so distant
So we won't be so isolated, segregated and separated
Flick the switch and let's start fighting this wicked
And cruel world together to make things right

Instead of getting shot down by our own peers
We been apart for far too long
It would be nice to get black together again
We can't win the game if the game is fixed against us
We need team work
How many times, just this year alone
Have you seen brothers get locked down for fighting each other
Ifwe use our head, we wouldn't be fighting "at all"
We don't fight against flesh and blood
But against principalities, against powers
Against spiritual wickedness in high places
Against the rulers of darkness of this age
So let's unite, flick the switch, turn on some light
Choose to unite, in positive ways
United we stand, divided we fall
All for one and one for all, wake up, see the light
And you will be amazed
And that's why I wrote what you are about to read.

FLICK THE SWITCH, THE POWER IS ON

Oh happy days, oh happy days
When the saints go marching in
Most will be surprised, it'll be too late once they realize
"My God" it has been, a world wide
Revolution
When we unite and come together as one
The world will stop and stare
Some will stand in pride with nothing to hide
Some will commit suicide, and those who live, will live in fear
Behold how good and pleasant it is
For brothers to dwell in unity
Numbers is power, knowledge is power
Divide and conquer has been a successful strategy
So we need to come together in peace and unity
We have been divided for far too long
(flick the switch, the power is on)
It's time to come together and stand strong
Too much blood shed, too much wrong
The wickedness of the world is on our shoulders
The look of frustration on my brothers face
Let's come together as one, my brothers
And heal the open wounds
That has infected our race
A house that is divided can never stand
We will either stand together strong
Or build our house in the sand
You might be saying to yourself
What I'm talking about won't change nothing
Ifyou are, then you are the one to blame
For our violent, self destruction (flick the switch, the power is on)

It's time to come together with no more hesitation
No only for ourselves but for the next generation
Why are we so quick to shed each others blood
And drag each other's name through the dirt and the mud
Talk about and doubt your brother
Tum state evidence and sell out each other
Could it be fear, envy, jealousy or just confusion
Hopeless, ignorant, brothers misusing
Each other in ways that are misunderstood
Or could it be the fact that you are the rat from way back
And still up to no good
It shouldn't take another civil rights riot to have success
How many black leaders do we have to lay to rest
Before we clean up
Before we wake up and stop settling for less
(flick the switch, the power is on)
It's coming to you live
"it's not transmitting", "it's not televised"
We are not on the air, the power is out
If the enemy is not within my friend
Then what's all the peer pressure about
Ifwe came together in perfect harmony
Then what would they have to say about us
Then what would their excuses be
Ifwe came together in perfect harmony
Then how many of our young will be in the cemetery or the penitentiary
Ifwe came together in perfect harmony
Just imagine the power, the peace and tranquility
Ifwe came together in perfect harmony
What would life be like in our community, ifwe came together in harmony
(flick the switch, the power is on)
Behold how good and pleasant it is for brothers
To dwell together in unity
It's like the precious ointment upon the head
That ran down the beard, even Aaron's beard
That went down the skirts of his garment
As the dew that descended upon the mountains of Zion
For there the Lord commanded the blessings
Even life forever more
Ifwe came together as one (the power is on, the power is on)
Oh happy days, oh happy days
When the saints go marching in
Most will be surprised
"My God", it's the revolution
Ifwe came together - ifwe came together
In peace and unity
It's not a sign of power
There's power in numbers my brother
One early morning you're going to "wake up"
Wipe your eyes and tum on your TV
And then you are going to realize

There is power in unity
The revolution is finally being televised
And all the little white lies are being exposed
"we are on the air again"
"the power is on" "the power is on"
And everybody knows, and everybody knows
The peer pressure is gone
We flicked and switched up
And now the power is on
Things are not what they used to be
Change has come through unity
We've silenced the violence and help up on crime
It sounds good and it's coming ull In good time
There's been an evaluation, a revolution
We've found another solution
Discrimination, segregation, it's not welcome in this nation
It's no longer an abomination for us to have an education
The states are united, "we are divided"
And everyone knows something is wrong
It's time to unite for what's right
(flick the switch, the power is on)
(the power is on) against police brutality, drug addiction and conspiracy
(the power is on) against the racist and the prejudice
(the power is on) for equal rights and opportunity
(the power is on) for fair trials in the court room
To shut down all the political deceivers
To stop the stereotype
And those who are out to mislead us, to stop us from doing right
Let's let the world know that these days of black on black crimes are gone
For we have flicked and switched up
Watch out world (the power's on) (the power's on)

There was once a time if one of your mothers friends or family saw you doing wrong, that they will give you a whipping, then when you got home you got another one
Now most of the same people that once disciplined the young, is buying drugs off of them.

President Reagan main focused was on sending billions of dollars on satellites, to put in orbit, he called it star wars.

From John Adams to the 35th president Kennedy, the focus was on arms and war.
George bush SR, said read my lips taxes will not go up, and as soon as he got in office, taxes went up.
William Clinton got busted committing fornication right in the white house.
And after George Bush told that lie, white America elected his son for president, for two terms
Anything but let a black man have the key
So rev Jessie Jackson, and rev Al Sharpton, didn't stand a chance, but was able to pave a way.

This country had many people that just didn't give a dam about the black man from the ghetto but to lock him in jail and keep him enslaved
It's a chest game and as long as the white king defeats the black king.

So when I graduated college I moved to Chicago to help lead a voter registration drive, I taught constitutional law at the university of Chicago, and remained active in my community
I wanted to unite all people around a political purpose
In the Illinois state senate I passed the first major ethics reform in 25 years.

I cut taxes for working families and expanded health care as a united state senator
I reached across the aisle to pass ground breaking lobbying reform.
Lock up the world's most dangerous weapons, and bring transparency to government by putting spending on line.

I ran a campaign and my slogan was called change we can
Just like my father and my forefathers, I believe in change, and I believe that times have changed dramatically.
Racism is not a thing of the past, know not by a long shot
But there are more decent people with loving heats today then in times past
And people are tired of being lied to, and stolen from.

There are more black governors and senators today then in history of man kind
And if 43 white men couldn't fix this system, without putting the country in more and more in dept.
Then maybe it's time for a black man to have the key.
So I ran and on Nov 4th 2008 I was elected, the first black man in history to be elected for presidency in the united states.

I was confident that I stood a good chance, after all the hate crimes in south Africa
A man by the name of Mandela who was in prison for over 20 years got out and became the president of the mother land Africa, so I kept moving forward too.
And even though the republican party was strong, there was to many people who lost loved ones in war, and no one wanted to see another one.

One of the fears was seeing that my Sen. McCain fought in the war and was proud of it
No one wanted to see more unnecessary blood shed.
Besides we wanted to get our troops back home from Afghanistan were bush left them
I had my debates and held my campaign.
on jan 20th 2009 I was sworn in as the 44th president of the united states.

Most people say we got a long way to go, how long before we make it, we just don't know
But ant know stopping us now.

The song was being sung

We went from being the worst thing that you can call a human being, a nigger
 Something lower then a dog, to the most powerful person in the united states of America.

"The world won't get know better, if we just let it be"

The song we need to sing

CHAPTER 16: UNITED AS ONE

I ONCE WAS BLIND
BUT NOWI SEE
THE FUTURE LOOKS GOOD FOR EVERY MAN

Looking at life through the eyes of a child
With faith and joy and a gentle smile
But as I grow older and become a man
The racism, the hate, I could never understand
Discrimination and segregation, society and racial tension
The white house war against the poor
Republicans, blacks and Christians
I once was blind but now I see
Private prisoners, house maids, and home slaves
Fire, brimstone and the horrors of hell
Descendents of slaves, the violence and silence
And things we were made never to tell
Walking in darkness seeking the light
Mississippi River lead me on
Beyond the sorrow, hate and death
Beyond the plantation where I was born
I can see the trails of blood from Washington, DC
The lynching and tension in Memphis, TN
The Birmingham scam
The raping and hating in slavery
The things we were robbed of
The things we were giving
The will power that kept us wanting to keep living
The tragic mistakes and violent outbreaks
We still stand with pride and loyalty of kings
In broken slave chains and poor people's campaigns
The demand is high to pioneer another coalition
To organize a committee particularly
For those who are blind and for those who will listen
I once was blind but now I see
The land of the rich, the land of the free
And the foolish scams you've played on me
Held down by political conspiracy
Ruler of darkness and powerful liars
With hidden tactics to create invisible chains
To hold us back and keep us struggling
Like pieces in a chess game
From Queen Elizabeth to King James
From the white house castle
To the smallest pawn
You will be conquered
And life will go on
So the revolution "will be" televised
When the world sees through your foolish lies

And all your social organizations of bigotry
Will come tumbling down
Like a Mississippi Valley
What the devil means for bad, God means for good
One day we will all understand
I once was blind, but now I see
The future looks good for every man.

UNITED AS ONE

Some truth, some fiction
The names have been changed in this story to protect the innocent
But the message is a strong one, and those that read this book with an open mind would
understand what's being said.
Know it ant over by a long shot, but we came a long way and this is how we got here
So no matter how rich you are, or educated you get, never forget were you come from.

In remembrance of those who gave their lives so we can live
To those that paved the way, for this day of glory to come.

Even though 40 acres and a mule, won't make up for, the injustice that has been inflicted upon
us for a life of hate death and torture.
To have a black president is a great gift from heaven
And a reword to all those who know the pain
We came, we saw, and we concord.

All through America, grave yards of dead slaves, men women, and children.
 If Each skeleton can talk, what do you think they would say about our generation ?
The way we walk, talk, and treat each other, the stress, and lack of progress, Peace, and war,
and what 'they 'died for.
The things we take for granted
The things we should appreciate
The presidential debate
And how we should collaborate
Were we got our strength from
And who we should give credit to
The importance of keeping our family together
Who to love, and how to
How they overcame
and how we can over come
I believe that they would say
Just stay united as one.

CHAPTER 17: POEM, I SHINE

I SHINE

I am a tree that cannot be cut down
Im a stone which chipped off of a rock
Created on a mighty mountain
Im a seed planted on good ground
A water fall springing from a holy fountain
Im the son of mother earth
I've been blessed since birth
And im gentle as an exotic flower
And like a bright and morning star
I shine
I strike like lightning
And I can roar like thunder
With the power of a mighty rushing wind
And as pure as crystal
I shine
I've been a king
The leader of mighty tribes
I've been a slave the victim of being bribed
I've been perplexed
Separated
Hated and segregated
And still like a rich peace of coal
I shine
I've been a soldier in the constant battle called genocide
I've been a subjected in politics where I've been paralyzed
I've lived in the way of many cultures and survived
Laws have been made to hold me down
Many graves have been filled in the ground
I stand in a crowd and not make a sound
And still I shine
I've been called hymie
Piccananny
Nigger negro
Afro American
Even been called black
I've been shut out
Kicked out
With out
Bared out
And never welcomed back
And still like glitter in the eyes of a joyful child
I shine
From the elements of the mother
To the character of the father
From the joining of a brother to the death of another
Even though I may suffer

I shine
As long as the lord is my Sheppard
And I'm of sound mind
This little light is gonna be alright
Because I'm gonna let it shine "

Chapter 18: We Are the President

I CAN SUCCEED

I can be successful
I can overcome
One day at a time
Victory shall be mine
To stand and say I won
Iowe it to myself, for the joy I have enhanced
To treat myselfgood
Like I've always should
And to give myself a chance
And if I ever fall
Or make a small mistake
I dust myself off the best way I can
I'll do whatever it takes
Cause I can be successful
As any other man
I don't have to settle
For the lower level
Over and over again
I can learn to love myself
And to treat myself with respect
And not run away
Or wake up the next day
In jail with shame and regret
I can be successful
Clean and serene
I don't have to be high to succeed
I'll humble myself
And ask someone else
To give me to the tools that I need
No more dirty floors
Or sleeping outdoors
Or ripping and running for days
No more selling myself short
With no support
And taking chances with AIDS
Cause I can be successful
I believe in change
I can face life's problems and fears
I don't have to stuff my feelings and get high
I can face them and cry
Blow my nose and wipe away my tears
I'd rather wipe my face
Then to live in a place
Like prison or six feet under
Like a man should
Than to be institutional and wonder

If I could change
Can lover come
Would victory be mine
Would I have ever one
Could I point and blame someone else
What would be the blame
Booze and cocaine
For the things that I've done to myself
The choice is mine
And that's guaranteed
The ball is in my hand
To fail or succeed
Or even give it a try
Yet I can succeed
It's also guaranteed
If I don't try
The chances are great
I would die
I have a right to be happy
A need to be content
A want to stop inflicting
Self-punishment
Compassion
And aggression, mixed emotions
Is it me
The consequences are too hard to bear
I looked yet could not find
The one's I left behind
And those who are here don't care
So with angry energy
I fight to be free
From this wicked addicted behavior
For the drugs that penetrated my mind
And motivated my life in time
Became my Lord and my savior
I can murder and hide
Or commit suicide
My life is one big problem
Or I can learn the rules
Pick up the tools
Work on my problems and solve them
Why settle for less
When I can do my best
For what is guaranteed
After my whole life
Was a senseless sacrifice
"Finally I can succeed"

WE ARE THE PRESIDENT

Now that we have a black president can we still play the blame game, for the injustices that's happening today.
Well the smoke hasn't cleared yet to the fullest
It's still gonna take a lot of time before things truly change.

The president can only do so much, he has to answer to congress for the decisions he makes
And congress is white people who has to be convinced to the changes that he is willing to make
We have a president who is not just looking out for one race of people.

We have a president who is trying to do good for the whole country
And that's a great thing.
But what are we going to do as a people to take care of our selves
The crime rate is still increasing, black on black crime is still at a great high, and that's a problem.

NO BLAME - NO SHAME

I was raised in a project on welfare
My mother was the only one that did care
I used to steal bikes just to have one
I used to jack other kids just for fun
I never had anyone to look up to
But the players on the comer and the drug crew
I used to go to gas stations for a job
But my address in the project made it hard
I saw Super Fly at the movies
He had a style of his own, that moved me
So I turned into a stick-up kid
And I tried to have everything that Super Fly did
I've been in and out of jail all my life
The game I was playing had set dice
It's just a check mate, no win situation
I even started taking medication
Cause the white man told me I ain't right
And according to his world, I'm a parasite
So I went to seek help from the black man
If no one can't, my Own will understand
A brother tried to kill me cause I was on his block
I guess he thought I tried to stick him for a white rock
If everybody is blind, who can see
Man, this peer pressure is killing me
Even among my own there's segregation
That's what the white man wants, separation
Like a puzzle of the world with an extra piece
Round and round it goes, just never cease
In and out, up and down, and around again

Looking for a space on this puzzle for a young black man
Where else in this world would I fit
Besides jailor the war zone project
So I became somebody when I joined a gang
We had our own block and respect for our name
I had money every day, made it day and night
I had more than the white man and I'm a parasite
They just got more troops, but it's all the same
Sometimes I reminisce on the past
I think about stealing bikes and I laugh
My cousins that were raised in the suburbs
They wouldn't touch a drink nor smoke herb
One even got a job as a policeman
Is there a piece in this puzzle for an African
My cousin is a cop and I don't doubt
That he will cuff me up too cause he's a sell out
My life was always hard and full of shit
Now I'm just the black man from the projects
Now I sit in a jail cell and try to fight
A system that considers me a parasite
The doctors want to give me medication
Another check mate in a no win situation
So I try to make changes that are right
Like go to church on Sunday and Wednesday nights
But the picture shows Jesus as white
How can a black brother get tight
With a white picture that never did care
For a black man from the project on welfare
So I pray to Jesus who is not white nor black
And I patiently wait for him to come back
And forgive me for believing the lie
That I can live and die like Super Fly
The world is not a puzzle, it's a painting
It's not the white man, it's Satan
It don't matter where you're from, it's where you're at
Don't do what I did, just learn from that
Now the morale to my story is clear
You can make it out of the project, off welfare
But if you take the wrong road like I did
There's a casket or a jail cell waiting for you kid
Don't be hard headed, take my advice
Don't blame another man for what you did in life
Believe in God and never forget to pray
Life is what you make of it and crime doesn't pay
It doesn't matter where you are from but where you are at
And you can be someone others can look up to, believe that
And don't get caught up in all that racist, systematic
Shift the blame shit
If they make it from the suburbs
YOU can make if from the projects

NO BLAME
NO SHAME

69

THE LAND OF MILK AND HONEY

The year is not over yet, it is Sept 2009 and there has been 35 black on black shootings in Boston alone.
I can only imagine what it may feel like for a parent to lay to rest their child, that was killed by the hands of another black person.
Most young black men in the inner cities are drug dealers or drug addicts
There are a lot of nice cars on the streets in the inner city.

Looking at the owners I can't understand, how a poor person can afford such a nice car
The reality is that most people in these neighborhoods are on welfare
Why don't they focus on houses and land?
Something more concrete to leave to their children.

For the most part, black people are being stereotyped now more than ever
It's so bad that we even stereotype each other, some brothers really truly want to work, but can't get know job.
Why? Maybe they are not trusted, or maybe there lazy and don't want to work
Or maybe they made some mistakes and broke laws at a young age, and when they apply they tell the truth on the application 'have you ever committed a felony
And then get denied, high school diploma or not.
They see the power and respect, they get in the community when they have something to offer some one .

Maybe they want to feel needed or wanted, so they become drug dealers
Why not, they have their own business, set their own hours, and there making money
They play the hand that life dealt them.

Mothers are using drugs with their children, or children selling drugs to their parents
Most of our young are raising their selves, due to the fact that daddy is in jail or strung out
Or mom may even be so strung out, that when you see her, she's either, drunk, high, or on the streets selling her body.
Then she gets caught up, now she is using to forget, and getting high makes the pain go away for a short time.
The consequences are, the chess game is still being played
the prison system is still overflowing with young black men doing time for violent crimes.
And the word nigger has become street slang, it's so bad that black people are calling each other that wicked name willingly without thought.

the system has brainwash and corrupted the mind of young black people so bad, that we are lynching each other in many different ways, but who cares

we got our own people putting each other in jail, or shall I say slavery.
Slavery because the government gives the states and counties more money for more prisons to be built.

It got so bad at one time that governor wells was asking for so much money from president Bush for prison reform, that the president respond was, why don't you just build a wall around the whole city?

40 thousand a year for each inmate
Laws have been made to hold us down
Strict and stiffer sentencing, the more time a young black man spins in prison the more money demanded.
So the more young black men that gets convicted and sentenced, the more money the state gets.
While foreigners come to these states from all other countries
Labeled as residence or citizens, getting these visa's, grants and bank loans
Opening up businesses in our community, we even rent apartments from such one's, while we struggle on welfare.
The only businesses we seem to be able to run are, hair salons, or barbershops, even then were renting from someone that had nothing to do with laying the foundation of this land
In slaved for four hundred and thirty five years.

Sure you can say that other nationalities was enslaved to, but never in the history of mankind
Have any other nationality suffered the way we did
More slaves were killed in one year than in the whole Jewish holocaust
At least the Jewish community got something back
What did we get, but a promise for 40 acres and a mule, an apology from president Clinton
welfare or maybe social security, there's still know equal opportunities in the work force
And it was slavery that made America such a great country.
Slaves were the computers of yesterday
You program something into them and they did it
Weather it was work or entertainment, free labor ect..
Blacks have struggled all their lives
Constantly reaching for the sky, from ground level

Some even try to get out of the hood, just to try and live good, without having to lock their doors at night, or worry about someone steeling their babies bike.
Thinking if they move away that maybe they can make a way
Just to find isolation, stereo types, still being looked down on and miss judged.
And God forbid if they commit a crime and get time
Just for being black and up to know good, in the wrong neighborhood

You get double the amount of time you would have got in the city.
So we get in were we fit in, "the hood"
Trying to make the best of what little we got
On the streets of death
Were families fall apart.

CHAPTER 19: AMERICA'S CRIME AND PUNISHMENT

IT'S AMERICA'S
CRIME AND PUNISHMENT

There's a job to be done
For everyone
Loyal citizens fear not
For now is the time
To make up your mind
And face these problems we've got
I'm trying to remember
The crime I committed
I was so drunk and high, I forgot
The room was cool but the street was very hot
The task was difficult and the odds was against me
How can I fulfill my cravings, feed this monkey on my back
And remain free
It's a bad time of the day for money to come my way
And man this monkey is VERY GREEDY
Not in despair but to be whole and complete
To bring a better day for myself
As the monkey on my back started to attack
No dope, no coke, no wealth
And as good a friend he won't let me depend
On no one but myself
So I committed a crime, went to court and got time
America's solution - prison and pain
I didn't give no struggle
I didn't want no trouble
I just wanted more dope and cocaine
Is prison the solution
For my confusion
And burning desire for rocks
The court could have
Sent me to rehab
Or even a state detox
And now I must stay
Locked down this way
For a crime I don't remember, or no if I did
And within these walls
The tear drops fall
Going through withdrawals
Curled up like a little kid
Isn't that histatic
An unmanageable addict
The world's largest state convict
No methadone line
Or rehab time
IT'S PRISON
America's crime
America's punishment

AMERICA'S CRIME AND PUNISHMENT

We live in low class places that they use to call the projects the ghettos of yesterday, but because they did a little renovation, they call these same old run down places housing complexes or developments.
Put a coat of paint on a building and change the name, but it's all the same
the same old struggle.

Some rap music has degraded our sisters, by calling them bitches and whores
the lost generation with no one to look up to.
The white man is stealing our music, and their children now want to dress, dance, and talk like black children.
While they are trying to imitate our style, we are trying to be more white.
We can't stand the texture of our natural hair
Selling cosmetic lies have become a well paid industry
Some even wear contacts to change the color of their eyes.

Black cops teaming up with white cops, playing the same old deadly games that white cops have always played on blacks.
Some were along the line they confused murder, with serve and protect.

The only time a young black man from the projects can get any kind of social respect, is if he becomes a police officer or make it to be a professional athlete.
Instead of slaves being sold off, they have child welfare or d-s-s the department of social services, taking children from their families at will.
In most cases its neglect, which at some point its understanding
But the rat is always going to go for the cheese, even in a maze.
So if you keep poor black folks in a community with drugs and liquor stores on every corner
Eventually someone is going to try something.
And then the disease is passed down from generation to generation
It's a chess game, called kill the black king, if the head is cut off, the whole body will die
And with that being done puts a great strain on the black women as well.

BLACK WOMEN RISE
BE STRONG AND SURVIVE

Life is a death trap, where only the strong can survive
Remember politics and Watergate, stealing and selling lies
Having the best in life is nothing if it brings out the worst in you
So how can you sit and judge me when you do the same things I do?
A lawyer gets caught for embezzlement
A DA gets busted taking bribes
Police are out getting high

And the FBI are steadily telling lies
And stands a young brother like me
With a dream to be all I an be
But afraid to fall in love
'cause I might not land on my feet
Black women I know, life is hard
And rent is always short
Your man's injail but he knows how you feel
We all can use a little support
He dreams of making love to you
To have all of you to himself
While he fantasizes about you in his mind
You're making love to someone else
Don't kick him to the curb
And leave him in the street
He's not a cat so don't throw him like that
'cause he might not land on his feet
Remember the times of old when we were loyal till death did us part
From the cotton field to the slop we ate, yet nothing broke our hearts
Are you so brain washed, mentally lost, watered down and weak
To take a man to court for child support
With a restraining order to keep him in the street
We once ran from the slave man, didn't know where we was going but made it here
Now you run to the slave man from me, claiming to be in fear
Life is a death trap, where only the strong can survive
I don't say this to put you down
But to open your eyes to realize
A farmer's best crop is fertilized in the best shit
And we've had our shit in life
Black woman, my queen, I pray that we can rise again
And stop calling me a nigger, acting like the slave man
So many people got lynched and hung for the things we take for granted
Some committed suicide cause they just couldn't stand it
Stand by your man black woman and he will stand by you
And once you start to count your blessings you will see that dreams do come true
I got calluses on my hands, pain in my heart and fire in my eyes
We've been through a lot but only the strong can survive
Black women, I know life is hard
You take care of your children and pray to'God
You need a man standing firm on his own
Someone you can call the head of the home
Ignorance comes in all nationalities
And close friends can be the worst enemies
We all got the world on our back
We just suffer cause we're black
And if a man had a woman's support
We can overcome that 'fact'
Black women, stand on your feet
I know it's hard on the street
Living in danger ain't no game
A young black man in a casket, such a shame

Who's gonna pay for his tombstone
A young black mother broke and all alone
They're sending people to the moon, that's good
But they can't keep drugs out of the neighborhood
Black women, open your eyes, watch the sun rise
And realize, use your head and be wise
Cause only the strong can survive
Never be ashamed of what you are
And always be all you can be
But you can't be all that
Unless you be with me
Cause I'm a young black man making it
Not like the man who's faking it
Life is hard and I hate it
But only the strong can survive.

Most black woman are trying their best to raise the family alone
We was taught as slaves to produce children for our masters sake, so he can increase his inventory.
Today we do the same thing, most black men have children all through the city by many different woman
Players, imps or whatever they call their self
the reality is most of them end up inmates or dead
And the women is left to face this unfair selfish world alone.
Some find there escape in booze or drugs, becoming dealers or prostitutes, then inmates in prison.
Most black people get out of jail and go right back to the same old behavior, to end up back in prison.
It's what I call a vicious cycle
There are more black woman dying from sexual transmitted deceases then cancer.
There are more black men dying from black on black crimes then sexual diseases.

Do we still need the k-k-k to kill us or to stop us from getting a education
know' because the wily lynch syndrome has infected our people so bad that now all the white man has to do is stereo type the black man put him in jail, sit back and watch the evilness unfold.

We were once people of royalty, descendents of African kings
We still have the desire to stand for something, to become something.
But we take that positive energy, and turn it to negative energy
We take that God giving natural spirit, and use it with evil intentions.
Most of us don't even know who we are or where we come from
So with good intentions I hope this book will open up our mind to think 'Cabbala'.

CHAPTER 20: THE METAMORPHOSES

THE HUMAN TOUCH

You can fight my wars, get right up there, on the front line
But don't touch me
I'll watch you play basketball
But don't you touch me
I'll watch you play football
But don't you touch me
I'll cheer you on, you can be my favorite player
But don't you touch me
I'll watch you fight, even call you champ, my champ, the people's champ
But don't you touch me
I'll eat your cooking, teach me how to cook that good old soul food
But don't you touch me
We can talk but you have to agree with me, don't you be too aggressive
We can look at each other, not too much eye contact, I'll listen to your music
But don't you touch me
Clean my house, wash my car, teach me how to dance
Shop at my store, give your money
But don't you ever touch me, without my consent
OK, I'll shake your hand, you have done a good job
But that's it, only a handshake
Don't pat me on the back, don't come around me after dark
You and your kind stay away, or I'll call the police, you understand
Stay away, don't move into my neighborhood, and most of all, don't you touch me
"News Flash" "News Flash" "Today's top story"
A young white male was struck by a car tonight
He lost a lot of blood and needed a blood transfusion
The hospitals only Afro-American doctor performed
An outstanding open heart operation
When the young white man awakened
He also agreed to the doctors professional performance
As the young white male sat there
With tears in his eyes
Not knowing that the blood donor was also black
....the black man's blood saved his life
Told the doctor that he had done a fine job
The doctor then said, "1 could not have done it by myself'
"You also have a strong will to live"
The white male slowly put his head down
With a little smile on his face
And with a small gentle heart, he then said,
"THANK YOU, I'M TOUCHED"

THE METAMORPHOSES

What is this new breed of race, ? that is carrying the blood of all nations
that evolved from so much hard ship, from hate and slavery

Decedents of kings and queens.

It all started with the mother land Africa, then all other nationalities from Indian, to Cuba to
Asia, from Egypt to French, German and Irish, a mixer of all races
Even the white man has a large mixer of blood
And the same countries we go to war to kill, Is our of spring.

Maybe God, knowing the future, knew that he had to allow our blood to be mixed
So we can become, like Jesus the savior of the world
The only difference is we are free marked angels with a sinful nature.

With freedom of choice, its ungodly, but we choose to sin, to kill, to destroy
But where did we get that sinful nature from?

We once lived in perfect hominy with our God, then came the devil and destroyed every thing
And when cane destroyed able, the violence began.
Yet God has shown his love, mercy and forgiveness, to us in such a powerful way
That he gave us a way out 'cabbala' think'

Can you feel in your soul, and know that God has been watching over you
Guiding and protecting you, and even though you have done wrong, and made bad choices in
life, he has forgiven you, simply because you asked him to.

Have you ever felt that you are, who you are, because many on your family tree had your same
personality, and spirit.
Have you ever looked at your children even your grand children and saw yourself.
Have you ever stood in a crowd, and gave off a since of kingship just by your presence
And even though your poor, the world looks up to you 'WHY'

Cabbala 'think'

no matter where you go in the whole world, we are there
Yet still have the dominant seed to remain its natural color
Skin like brass, hair like wool.
 walking with the spirit of its creator, like a dance with rhythm
Why is all the evil forces of the enemy constantly trying to kill us, and make us suffer
With the spirit of our ancestors we have fought a good fight, we have struggled, and we have
risen
We are survivors.
We are Adam and we are eve
We are Shem, Ham, and Japheth

We are mosses
We are martin, we are Malcolm
 we are African
we are Nubian
We are kings and queens
we are royalty
we are worriers
we are conquerors
 We are leaders
We are alive
we are strong, African Americans
WE ARE ALL RACES MIXED INTO ONE
We are the alpha and the omega
We are like Gods
God's chosen people
 so act like it
And stand
Just because 'we are' we are!
Heaven sent, to Africa & made in America

Chapter 21: All 44 Presidents

HEAVENLY ARTIST

All mighty power, creator
Of all living things
The sun shines, the plants grow, the birds sing
In darkness the stars sparkle
The moon glows great light
The mountains, the waters, divided just right
The raindrops, the snowflakes, the rainbow
The whispering in the wind
The soul, the spirit and the heavens
Created by my creator
Of the earth and heavens above
God of peace, God of mercy, God of power, God of love
In the garden, my God created man
He molded me with sand and held him in his mighty hand
With the breath of life and all the love one can give
God created man in his image
A living soul, wonderfully made
By the most creative God
We live ....
We were made by Him, through Him and for Him
And without Him we cannot exist
Spoken into existence by the word of God
And gifted with life, molded in love, mighty creator
My heavenly artist.

ALL 44 PRESIDENTS

1st George Washington
2nd John Adams
3rd Thomas Jefferson
4th James Monroe
5th John Quincy Adams
6th Andrew Jackson
7th Martin van Buren
8th William Henry Harrison
9th John Tyler
10th James Knox Polk
11th Zachary Taylor
12th Millard Fillmore
13th Franklin Pierce
14th James Buchanan
16th Abraham Lincoln

17th Andrew Johnson
18th Ulysses S. Grant
19th Rutherford G. Hayes
20th James Garfield
21st Chester Arthur
22nd Grover Cleveland
23rd Benjamin Harrison
24th Grover Cleveland
25th William McKinley
26th Theodore Roosevelt
27th William Howard Taft
28th Woodrow Wilson
29th Warren Harding
30th Calvin Coolidge
31st Herbert Hoover
32nd Franklin D. Roosevelt
33rd Harry S. Truman
34th Dwight D. Eisenhower
35th John F. Kennedy
36th Lyndon Johnson
37th Richard Nixon
38th Gerald Ford
39th James Carter
40th Ronald Reagan
41st George H.W. Bush
42nd William J. Clinton
43rd George W. Bush
44th Barack H. Obama
after only nine months in office
He was awarded the Nobel peace prize
Some presidents have the people work for them
And others work for the people
Barack h. Obama is one who works for the people

IT'S NOT EASY BEING ME

Demons want to try me and deny me
Test the stress and then ride me
I always got to go that extra mile
Because you stereotype my style
I'm a genuine black man
On a spiritual level
Why you think we call you demons devil?

Cause you are slippery and slimy like a snake
You show no love and your smile is fake
The greed in your heart is for personal gain
To kill and make war in a righteous man's name
The things you have done and the things that you do
Is a prime and indecent, expression of you
As a man thinketh so is he
Like father like son, through history
Chain a man, hang a man, even lock him down
Work him, don't pay him, then lay him in the ground
Forever driven mad and viciously
And it's not easy to be me
Racism, separatism, hate crimes
From a mind of the demons
Money brackets, political tactics
From the mind of a schemer
From the White House Door
To the State House Floor
When can a black man have the key?
All in good time, what's on your mind?
Only for a political conspiracy
Racist demons, for those who don't know it
But your actions in life will always show it
They say times change but I can't see
And it's to easy to be me
You push me to check my attitude
And if I push back
I'm violent and rude
I don't' have ajob and you won't hire me
Affirmative action forces your hand
To fmd a man from another country
And call him 'minority'
And it's not easy being me
Allover the world
Throughout the nation
Stumbling blocks, trials and tribulation
I fight the demons, drugs and diseases
The devil trying to kill me
Have mercy Lord Jesus
There is something special
About the black man
One day we will fully understand
Why is the devil constantly trying to keep us oppressed?
Is it his vengeance on God?
Knowing we are blessed
Look at life today
Then study history
Then admit it to yourself
That you can see
The pressure, the reality
That it's not easy to be me

Demons want to try me, deny me
Test the stress and then ride me
I always got to go the extra mile
Because you stereotype my style
I'm a genuine black man
Caught up in a conspiracy
And it's not easy
No, it's not easy to be me.

No other president in history had to deal with the pressures of being the first one to concur
The peer pressures like the first black president.
To constantly be under the magnify class, and looked on with confusion
What is this new black president going to do? look out for his own people?
Who are his people?
He to walks with that heavenly mixer of blood line

Yet he didn't get into this war to be a hero
He just wants to make a change, a change that will benefit us all.
Everything from foreign exchanges, nuclear weapons, to bomb threats, racial hate, stimulus,
white supremacy, and we can't forget the political threats and the media circuses.

Trying to get the approval from liberals, whites blacks, republicans and democrats
Not to mention the deficit, just to name a few of his trials and tribulations.

He also fighting a war that has not been addressed but is in existence
That wile being in power he has never fought before.
In house threats, from haters, from those who still want to separate us
Traders, backbiters and manipulators, some of his own staff.

He understands that just because you're from another country
That don't make you our allies or enemy
See a good solder fights for his people
And in turn, his people will fight for him.
He holds the torch for every black man or women, that has it in them to run for president in
the future.
Put the weight of the country and your people on your back
And let's see how fore you will run.

But all great achievements arose from dissatisfaction, it takes a village to raise a child
It's going to take a nation to raise each country.
So he humbly tells us that he can't do it by him self
So the next question is, 'WHAT CAN WE DO TO HELP?'

Believe and achieve"
We alone decide the activities of the world
This is our destiny and we hold it in the palm of our hand.

The first step is to make changes in this system for equality all the way across the bored
To stop miss judging, prejudging, and putting each other down simply because of the color of
our skin.

A man by the name of john Dunn once said, and I quote, ;no man is a island entire if its self
So we must stop the hating and degrading, and separating.
We must teach the next generation to put in some participation, to make us all one nation.
We must stop playing that deadly chess game of genocide
Of selfishness and greed.
We need to stop looking at each other, as if one race is better than another
Stop the stereo type, miss judging and prejudging each other.

The time is going to come when there is going to be only one race 'the human race'
 the most potent seed is going to dominate.
 and the whole world is one day going to be people of one color
And as long as the devil rules your heart, there will be no peace.
Racism will continue to be passed down like a old recipe
 from generation to generation.

You see the names of all of the first 43 president, most was slave owners, who owned their own
plantations.
Then others owned house maids and home slaves.
Then we had a chosen few who understood the un holy conflict, and voted for freedom and
democracy.
So yes people can change, and change we can
And when the changes do come
We can do like the slaves did, what I spoke about in chapter 1
Sit back and feel the cool breeze after a hard day's work..

CHAPTER 22: THE WORLD IS YOURS

THE WORLD IS YOURS

It's important that young black men check
Their history and have a good understanding of self
Who they are, Where they are
How they got here and where they would like to go
Have a good understanding of God
Gods will and self, Gods will for self
If you can crawl, you can walk
If you can walk, you can run
As long as the rivers run
And the earth is by the rain and the sun
As long as the stars shine from the heavens
As long as the rivers run to the sea
You can be whatever you wish to be
You came too far in life and history
Run and faint not
If you want success
All you need to do is
"succeed"
The world is yours.

The greatest thing I have ever seen, was when black and white people came together in unity
To joined forces for a common cause for all mankind, From movie stars, to the everyday
common trash man.
To give honor to a great man, who had the courage to take a stand
To give honor to each other, for overcoming the biggest leap for all mankind
since the first man on the moon.
Since the invention of the wheel
 Since the discovery of fire
Since the coming of the Christ Jesus
 We the people, in the name of, Barack .H . Obama the 44th president of the strongest county
in the world the 'united' states of America.

You got my bishop and all my pawns
But I got your castle and I kept my queen
And defeated your king 'check mate game over"
Now let's face reality, and see life for just what it is, from the eyes of a child of God.

LIKE A CHILD OF GOD

As I sit in the dirt
I lean back on a tree
And wonder how many slaves hung here seeking to be free
I gaze upon the children, how they run, laugh and play
Not knowing the joys of being a child will slowly fade away
I think about the courtrooms, mankind and his greed
Where life is not a special thing nor is it guaranteed
I think about the system and how evil one can be
They give and take, the phony handshakes, and the threat of reality
I thought about the politicians and how they play the game
From one political lie, a whole nation could die, and yet they have no shame
Then a bird flew over my head and I wondered, was he free
Some have houses, some have cages, just like you and me
I could not find anything around that I can see that is free
The law of man, the law of nature, even gravity
Then I looked into the heavens and 1said to myself"gee"
After aU this time of working my mind, it was right in front of me
I'll just ask God, he sets captives free
The Bible says if I ask he will deliver me
So I prayed and asked the Lord, as I looked into the sky
A voice came down from heaven
It said, my son, do what I've done
Just take your cross and die
There is therefore no condemnation to those who walk in Christ
I don't mean suicide, I mean spiritual for life
The law of sin and death
No longer have a hold on me
For the law ofthe spirit oflife in Christ
Has set the captive free
As I sit in this dirt
I lean back on a tree
And wonder how many slaves just hung here
Seeking to be free
How many were set free, how many will realize
Just ask God
It's not hard for him to open your eyes
How many did accept him
How many did reject him
How many are still lost, how many just sat here, how many walked away
And those that found freedom in Christ, will run, laugh and play.

I remember tears filling the eyes of Oprah Winfrey and Jesse Jackson
They understood how far we've come as a people, as a nation
White people and black people feeling each other's pain.
From street hustlers, to talk show host, to single parents, and School teachers, and trash men.

telling their children that they can be whatever they put their mind to

Even the president of the united states of America.

All was there to see history in the making
A rainbow of colors in unity, lifting up change in the world

THERE FOR BLACK WHITE
AND FROM ALL WALKS OF LIFE
"WE ARE PRESIDENT"
And as we govern ourselves, we govern the world.

what's going to happen 4 years from now ?
Will he be reelected or rejected

The president of whom they said freed the slaves once said, and I quote
"If I had 8 hours to chop down a tree
I'll spend the first 6 sharpening my ax"

We have tried everything in all sides of the nationalities, to figure out what we may need to
make America a better place to live.
We have tried war, welfare, money tactics, more war, hate, genocide, murder, blame, bringing
people over from other countries and calling the residents even citizens.

we have tried everything, and nothing worked
The answer was right in front of our face.
The beetles wrote a song about it and I quote
"All we needed is love, love is all we need"

God is love, and love is all we need
A genuine love for all man kind
And finally we have started to sharpen up our axes
To cut down the tree of bigotry
Hate, race crimes, genocide'
And instead of just being alive
there are things we regret, and things we need to admit
We regret, the foolishness of our pass
We admit, that all mankind is from one blood line
So am I my brother's keeper ?
'YES I AM '
We have seen enough death
To understand the value of life.

So if we keep on killing one another
Then who are we going to turn to 'brother'

WE ARE THE PRESIDENT

WHO ARE WE GOING TO TURN TO BROTHER

Political action and affirmative action
Genocide is what we're doing to each other
And for ever more, were killing each other

sell out uncle tom house nigger
Master say shoot and you can't wait to pull the trigger

The jail house is full of brothers doing time
And the grave yards are overloaded from black on black crime

Fellers out snitching for a personal gain
Some are truly guilty and some have been framed

Some are selling out to climb the corporate ladder
We can blame the white man but it really doesn't matter

Cause were killing one another anyways
Guns, drugs, dirty needles and aids

From high school dreams to political schemes
From the church hall to the city hall

He who represents has a fool for a client

And a independent man is not reliant

In a world of the rich getting richer
And the poor one day away from poverty

I stand in a battle from all four sides
Stabbed in the back by the black, and the whit got me paralyzed

You don't have to be black to be a nigger
You don't have to be black to be a nigger

Ignorance come in all nationalities
If we are all equivalent then
why kill one another in greed

Living in hell, looking to heaven
Dreaming to escape to another place
Cause America was built on blood shed
Killing fir the cheese in a rat race

I didn't understand what they meant
When they said we will never have a black president

When I said have faith they looked at me strange
Cause I knew one day things had to change

Republicans, democrats, whites and blacks
Lawyers, judges police and crooks
Some steel from the government
 and some snatch pocket books

Some flip paper from a sky scraper
Some make their pay
from the alley way

Some may struggle on welfare
Some are getting high and some don't care

Some are in suits and some are in rags
Some swear with a oath that they respect their badge

 Some will kill you for just stepping on their shoes
Life is so hard they ant got nothing to lose

Some wont higher you, and will lie to you right in your face
You ask for direction and get sent all over the place

Who we are we going to turn to brother
The man on the corner dealing rock
Who will shoot you cause your on his block

Or the man that didn't come from the ghetto
Who's skin is black but he don't know

Some will just kill you out of pride
It's nothing personal, its genocide

It's time to come together cause we're all we got
If we don't take a stand we'll fall apart

The jail house is full of brothers doing time
And the grave yard is over loaded from black on black crime

Its genocide and the only way to win the fight
Is to silence the violence and unite

Cause if we keep on killing one another
THEN WHO ARE WE GOING TO TURN TO 'BROTHER'

A seed must die for a plant to grow
We have seen enough death to respect the value of life
It takes more energy to hate, then it does to love
Today's youth are tomorrows adults

And those that hate are a dying breed
So let's look forward for a better tomorrow
Because change is what we need

WE ARE THE PRESIDENT
Of the 'united' the united states
It's time to come together and live in peace
As ordinary people

91

You got to get over the Hump !!

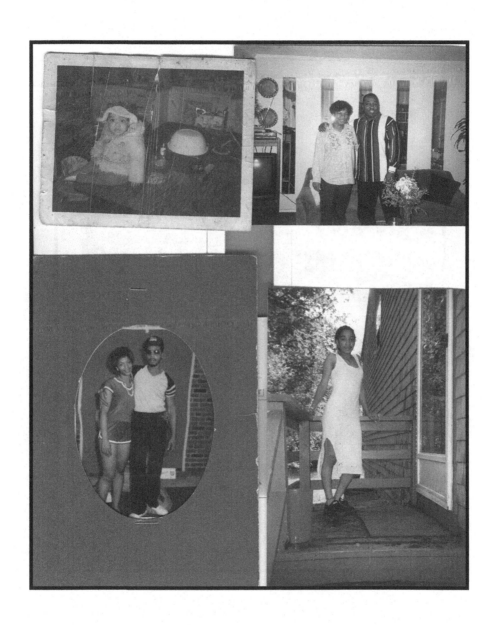

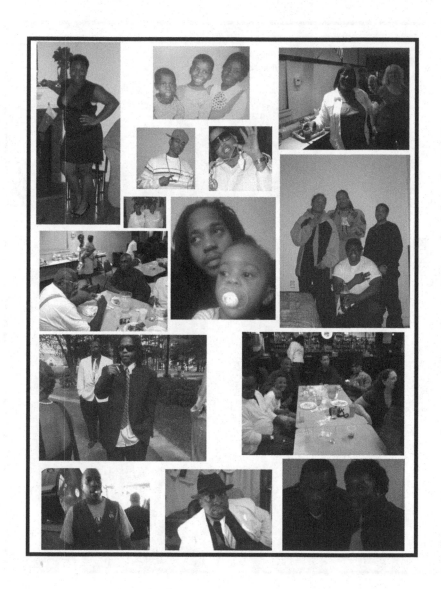

94

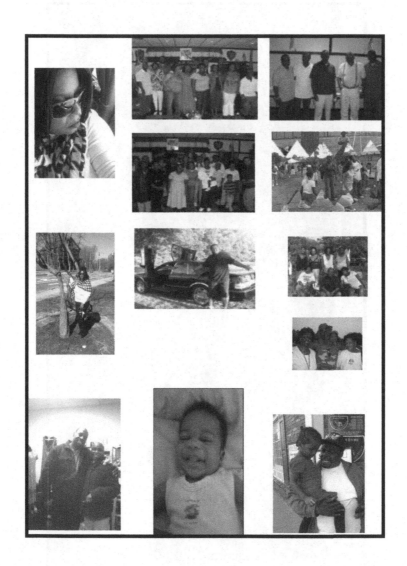

SO HOW CAN WE WIN?

it's not whether you win or lose but how you play the game

*the problem is games, there has been political games that
kept us in war for years
the street games, that has shed so much innocent blood
the judicial games that locks innocent men up
the marital games, a constant tug of war
the mind games that sent subliminal messages to the mind
a sign of hypnoses, that keeps this division
the economic games that keeps us struggling
and then we have the card game, when you play the race
card, you're a automatic winner, especially in politics*

*someone once told me if they had a million dollars, that they
will be successful
the world leads us to believe that success, is how much money
one has
the game of monopoly has taught us that if we buy and own
everything then we win
success is not how much financial support one has
success is how much family support one has
if you look through history, you would find that there were
many rich men who died old un happy and lonely*

*sure people are going to let us down, to every action there is a
reaction
it's not what others do, but how you respond to what others do
that makes the difference
if you are in a relationship and you truly love each other
then the color of your skin shouldn't matter, so don't pay know
attention to those outside of your marriage with their little
judgmental, nosey self centered ways
everyone has Disagreements, it's how you handle your
disagreements that matters, if you call your family for financial
help, and they don't pay you know mind
but when you call them, when you have a disagreement with
your spouse, and then they have no problem with getting
all up in your relationship, causing division and giving bad
advise
but yet she calls, every time she has a disagreement
especially when they come around acting all high and mighty
like they don't have no problems in their relationships
and like a fool you call them and complain
stop the madness, handle your own marriage, and stop
putting all these people in it
know more games speak from the heart, and express your
feelings in a calm way
not every mirage is going to work
most black women got so much baggage from there pass*

that they have a tendency of taking it out on the closest ones
to them
some black women have grown up in dysfunctional homes
some have been raped, some have been finically and
mentally abused
ex drug addicts and prostitutes, with big problems
it's hard to try and please and satisfy some one,
that's never pleased and satisfied

if you want your relationship to work learn to love each other
just the way you are
see our problem is, we are constantly trying to change others
and judging our partners, that we take the focus off of our self
how can you tell me my back yard has trash in it
when your whole house is dirty
once we stop sweeping our own dirt under the rug
and stop judging others for there's then maybe we will stand a
chance
the world is a scary place, we got people starving in some
countries
and in other countries they are having religious wars
the foolishness of mankind is we Got people praying to win a
war against people of their same faith
we got people hating each other, for the simple fact of the
color of their skin, yet we go to church and we pray for peace
it's called hypocrisy
Michael Jackson said it right
and I quote I if you want to make the world a better place I
I take a look at yourself and make that change'

first we must learn to love our self
then learn to love each other

love each other just the way they are
love all human beings as Gods children
in spite of the color of their skin or back ground
the world is full of Christians and religious people

be what you say you are, and then maybe

we can live in peace

CHAPTER 23: THE RESURRECTION

**THIS IS A STORY ABOUT THE FIRST BLACK PRESIDENT
IN SOUTH AFRICA
HIS STRUGGLES AND ACCOMPLISHMENTS
I CALL THIS STORY 'THE RESURRECTION'**

over 1, 000 Africans migrated south, living the best they can with what little they had
the white government had the power to make and change the laws of the land
many Africans had to make major changes in their lives
to live accordingly to the white man's ways, they all had to take on Christian names as well

there was a young man who took on the name nelson
he lived in a small village, in a hut made of grass
his father was a bolognas one who had five wives, and 9 children
they worked the fields and looked after live stock, they also hunt rabbits and birds
they was so poor they ate from one dish, the children had know toys to play with
so they would play with sticks, imagining that they was swords

nelsons mother sent him to school every day and nelson was eager to learn
one day he saw his father sick in bed with a bad cough, laying on his back
for days, sick and coughing, he even had a hard time holding down his food
one evening his father called for one of his wives, and asked her to bring him his smoke
pipe and his tobacco

nelsons mother said know, he don't need to be smoking in his condition
but nelsons father insisted, every one said know, then nelsons father demanded
his tobacco and pipe

they gave it to him, and he started to smoke, and then he started coughing real bad
then the pipe started to slowly drop, then he died

and that's how nelsons father died, in his sick bed smoking a pipe
at 9 years old nelson was sent away to be bought up by a chief
the other family was to raise him to be a king, that's what he was meant to be
he socialized, was taught by, and dealt with experts of his tribe
he was also taught as a worrier to fight in battle, with spires against gun powder
nelson lacked one thing to be an adviser for the chief
he needed higher education, so he was attended a school named clerkaberry
in fact when he got in office, he went back to that same school and mentored the
students

at 16 years of age he was taken to circumcision school
circumcision school is a African tradition, it is such a strong tradition that even in prison in
south Africa they circumcised each other
as soon as the person is cut he must say i am a man circumcision was a act of courage,
Horner, and respect

they would then burn the huts down, that you grew up in, as a symbol of one putting
their childhood behind them

then the chief would speak to them about man hood, and being a solder fighting for the
liberation of their people from the bondage of the laws and the system of the white man
nelson had to run to Johannesburg in the 1940's, he ran from a fix marriage
his cousin left with him
most Africans in Johannesburg worked in the mine's for little money
one day they was called for a meeting by an officer of the law, when they arrived they
was asked
who gave them permission to go to Johannesburg, they said the king
they was asked for their paper work that the king gave them
they said the king gave us permission to come here, then the officer pulled out a
telegram and said read this, it was a telegram from the king for the boys to return home
at once

at the age of 23, with no job and know money, nelson ended up in Alexander
it was a slum area outside if Johannesburg

most south Africans was not permitted to work in Johannesburg
a man by the name of Walter, who was a lawyer gave nelson a job as a clerk in his law
office, nelson was impressed over Walter, because he was black African and had a
professional business

Walter gave him a job as a clerk, and nelson went to school at night studying law
a big influence in nelsons life was a man named matambo, nelson learned allot from this man

nelson later married a lady by the name Evelyna in November
the south African prime minister was called in, he was a enemy in power to incinerate
black Africans

every day there was a symbol of a partite, if you didn't have your I-D on you
you was thrown in jail, and laws was passed to break family's
Mandela was appointed in June, 26 of 1950 to be the first volunteer to stand up and help
black Africans

and in 1953 Mandela opened his own law office, were he was known as being a good trial lawyer
he upset the police and the government, as well as the white public, when he cross examined white people

white people didn't want the people to govern, and share the country
the police would not let Mandela go to any events
nelson was away from home allot, he was always organizing and working for the people
, in 1957 nelson Mandela got a divorce

the police came to visit nelsons mother, and told her to stop her son from speaking politics or he would be found dead or thrown in jail
nelson had feelings for a lady named Winnie, so one day he called her and told her he wanted to see her

he spoke with a softness yet with authority so she listened, they started a relationship and a short while after that they was married
on December 1956 the police arrested 195 black Africans to try and keep them out of politics
the event was so popular, they gave the trials a name I the treason trials'
Mandela became a man with great respect and leadership
the focus seemed to be more on him and his followers during the treason trials
the government really didn't have any evidence, and there cases collapsed
and for 41/2 years the Africans continued to fight

one day while at a protest in front of the court house, the troops came in and opened fire on the crowds of black Africans

many was shot to death, the state then composed martial law
and made many laws to oppress black Africans

the law officials was told to arrest nelson immediately on site, dead or alive
he became to be a big threat to the white man and his laws

nelson wanted none violence just equality, so he addressed the government to meet with him and to address these problems, but there main focus was, how they can shut his mouth from persuading his people

the government would not sit down with the black Africans, instead the troops came in with their guns and violence and continued murdering people

Mandela left the country to try and raise funds, and to get military training for his people
when he returned he was arrested for leaving the country illegally
he was sentenced to five years, and was facing the death penalty for high treason
they locked up Mandela and his people, 'the Mandela's' was what they was labeled as
all he wanted democracy and equality, he was one who was willing to die for what he
believed in

he fought for all to live in hominy and peace, he fought against white domination
even from his jail cell, he got the word to his people and they was still obedient to his
words, and wouldn't act without his permission

Mandela and his comrades was sentenced to life in prison, the most hardest prison north
of cape town, it was like the living dead, waiting to be killed, like cattle
in prison they was treated like violent terrorist and radical people
one letter, one visit, every six months, it was a dangerous mission for Mandela to get his
words to his people, but he was patient and successful

in January 1965 they was addressed by the commissioner of state, and given hard labor
digging land with pitch folks and shovels
most of them would get punished after working sun up to sun down, they would punish
them for no reason

SING LORD AFRICA I SING NOW AFRICA I SING FOR THE PEOPLE

nelson was a good chest played, he was a patient man, sometimes it would take him 2
or 3 days to finish a game
they didn't have pin or paper, so they would right in the sand, when they was unable to
speak to each other

the last time he saw his mother, was when she came to visit him, then she died a short
time after, they constantly harassed his wife,
when his wife was arrested it bothered nelson allot, after 15 years in prison the law took
nelsons wife to a poor slum area and told her that's were you will live, this is your knew
home
and she survived and continued to carry the same message of her husband

the minister of foreign affairs said that there will 'never' be a one man, one vote, in Africa
the black Africans believed differently, they kept the faith that there will be and it would
be lead by nelson Mandela
the people will boy cart for nelsons freedom, ' free nelson Mandela I was a constant
chant
for over 21 years they continued to protest for nelsons freedom

nelson Mandela < prisoner 201282 > alive yet dead
after 7 years of a banishment Winnie Mandela was arrested for trying to return
she returned and started preaching to the people 'constitution revolution'

the government was willing to listen to people who wanted constitutional changes
but would not speak to people who wanted revolutionary changes
so speaking to nelson Mandela was out of the question

THE LIVING

Mandela is finally released after 25 years in prison
the black Africans never gave up on him or the movement
they continued to fight for their rights and for nelsons freedom
on February 11; 1990 he was released

a few months later Winnie Mandela was charged with murder
nelson stood by her as much as he could and continued to fight for the rights of his
people
and in 1992 Winnie was acquitted and released from the charges
the a-n-c had a little support, but wasn't recognized as a major force
the government continued to act in violence against black Africans
there was still more bombs, shootings, and murders

may 1990 Mandela became a strong political figure for the changes in south Africa
he spoke of a new nation of blacks and whites
but the government spoke against the n-c-s
in the attempted to stop the inauguration, the government continued with its acts of
violence
on April 1993 he received the Nobel peace prize
and even after that the violence still continued, even at a black African concert the
government come in shooting and killing innocent bystanders

Mandela spoke to millions of people on his campaign rally
people of all colors and walks of life was there, to support nelson
they bombed Mandela's election office
the I-F-P gorillas torched homes, and bombed cars, on march 28 Johannesburg
became a war zone, bloody violent out breaks was everywhere
the government did not want to make a peaceful election possible
on the 27th of April, the votes began at the poles
black Africans was voting for their first time
and south Africa had a new president
the inauguration briefing was meant to be a short one

on may 1994 was the inauguration for president nelson Mandela
the first black president of south Africa <back from the dead> and resurrected
from the dead cold prison cell, facing death, to the life that freed south Africa

'in remembrance of all of our brothers and sisters who died for the cause <we shall
overcome> you will always be remembered as freedom fighters, worriers, and hero's

CHAPTER 24: INTERRACIAL RELATIONSHIPS

A VIEW FROM A BLACK PROSPECTIVE
HOW CAN WE LIVE IN PEACE

some say that men go through menopause, and mood
changes, like women
i find that very hard to believe, due to the fact that I've had
allot of experience with women of all ages
do to the fact, i have twelve children, six boys six girls
and even if it is true, we don't go through it as bad as they do

I've never had sex relations with a women of my opposite race
but i do have family members who are married to such women

I've always felt that getting in were you fit in, was very
important
besides having to Measure up to the exceptions of her family
was something I was not willing to do, maybe Mr. Bo jangles,
but not me
so I've only dated and had relationships with black women
and I have always wondered' what make a black 'man' go
outside of his race, and treat a 'white women' like the 'queens
'that the sisters are, and should be treated like
some may say that people are people, and we all have the
same short comings
after my second marriage and the few relationships I've gone
through
I've found that there is no other human on this planet like a
black women
they would cook, and clean, and will take good care of you
they love their children, and they stay under pressure

they will also use and abuse you, and put you down every
minute of the day, but they claim to always love you
it's confusing to a man, that a women can show so much love
and affection
and have so many evil hateful ways, or maybe just trip out on
you without warning, say allot of things they really don't mean
and then expect you to be loving to them
you feel beet, and abused, then they want to make up
it's like Hitler asking the Jews to give him a hug

115

most hustlers and can men, learnt there traits from women
most children have to personalities, one of there mother, and
the other from their father
so one man could be genital and kind, and the same man
can leave you for dead, and not think twice about you
I want to blame the mix up and confused ways of most women
on slavery
because the black women has had it so hard, and even
today they are full of great fear so they act out, so the man
acts out

the difference between a black women and a white women is
if a black man gets caught cheating on a black women
the black women would kick him out of the house
cut up his clothes, or maybe even cut him, or slice his car tires

a white women would divorce you and leave you broke
and homeless, with no regrets
maybe even go as far as sleeping with one of his relatives to
get even

in the garden Adam was cool, he was walking the garden
talking with God, living in peace and at one with God
he named all the animals and spoke with them, and was
living in peace and hominy with his creator
then he got lonely and wanted eve, and that's when all the
problems started
don't get me wrong I love women, especially black women, if
you can find a women that would love and respect you
unselfishly, you got something good, white or black

but if you have a women that brings you more pain then
pleasure, then you have a problem, white or black

most men are runners, they have the tendency of running from
one problem to another, and if someone that they care
about hurts them bad enough, most men just leave
I remember watching a black child on the city bus, was being
bad, and his mom popped him, he looked at his mom with this
evil face, and went and sat in another row next to this white
couple

the message he was sending, was that if you don't treat me
right, I am going to get someone opposite of you too!

in other words, I've tried to work in your cotton fields
it was hot and sweaty, and I've tried to work loyally side by
side with you, all you ever did was talk down at me, and put
me down at all cost, with no empathy about my feelings
you never told me I did a good job, neither did you appreciate
me
so i am going over to work in the cool of the corn fields
were they talk respectfully to each other and help each other
in times of need,
and that's what the black man does, when he feels he is hurt
by the black women
he runs to the other field to find Peace, refuge and some one
who truly loves him for his hard work, and efforts.

so he ends up looking at the white women, because the black
women seems to be too demanding, head headed and out
spoken
besides subconsciously the black women seem to wants to be
white in other areas, like straitening her hair, coloring her eyes
and adopting that white look so much, why have a manikin,
when you could have the real thing?, why have some one
that's not excepted by society when you can have some one
that is?
why struggle all of your life as a black couple in a society that
miss judges you constantly?

so the black man has a relationship, even marries a white
women for all of these good things, just to find life even harder
most of society is not excepting interracial relationships

they have children who end up very confused
most of the immediate family even have their say of gossip
then he realizes that all women have the same old problems
just some greater than others
and he finds himself in a sad position, when he doesn't even
like himself, so he may drink or use drugs, not to face who he
really is
an unperfected self righteous man

or maybe he just goes on with his life, taking the good with the bad, in stride expecting the worst

whatever choices we make in life are on us, we make the bed that we lay in

the reality is that interracial relationships are becoming popular and there are more children today that have parents from two different ethnic backgrounds then ever in history
and one day it would be fully excepted
and as black people having the dominate seed, we are going to have more people of color then I since the beginning of time
then how would we be racist against each other
by the length of our hair, the size of our lips I the color of our eyes, or maybe by our complexion
we as mankind have a tendency of exulting our selves above others, for know other reason at all , but for the difference in which we have been created

for the most part the black man is not respected in society as a man
and when he gets home to the family that he suffers to support and they don't respect him either ,that could be trouble

he may even try to find many different ways to vent his anger sports, work music TV , or a bar stool, just to come home to a selfish ignorant flipped mouth women, that wants all he has to offer but don't want him
the most common thing that I hear that women say is
you don't understand my feelings ,or I want to talk about my feelings
they have a tendency of looking at the bad in the man
and the good in there self
when for the most part, its a sad thing when a young women takes on ant man to be in her children's life, just to have a babies daddy
most of the time the women may have a child or two
and 60% of the time the man, taking care of them ,is not the biological father
and yet he goes that second mile to make sure there worm in

the winter, and have clothes on there backs, even if he has to
go to some sort of public assistance for help ,were he has to
practically beg for the help needed
and he is still undermined ,degraded and put down by his so
called sister, his wife

the white man was born with the privilege of being a white
man in a white mans world
so he gets the bank loans and the other trustworthy attributes
the good jobs were he is served by those on low income status
then we have those T V shows that puts him in the light of being
a good family orientated man, police man; a fire man, a
doctor, someone with good morals and self confidence
so why wouldn't a black women wont a white man
if they was to have children by one then there children would
have the hair she always dreamed of having, know fake
extinctions, weaves, glue and all of those cosmetic lies

besides the black man is known as a jobless, drug addicted
jail bird, with no intentions on bettering his life

it's a little different when it's a white man with a black women,
then a black man with a white women
as long as the black man is not married to a white women or
have children by her his own people will except the
relationship
but as soon as he puts a ring on her finger, he is a sell out
when a white man judges the situation, he wonders, you mean
to tall me, she couldn't marry her own kind
to some its sleeping with a beast, a ape, or a gorilla, a slave,
and there children is a freak of nature
but to most, it's whatever floats your boat
others may label her to be a she devil, or the black mans
burden
or even the black man's trophy

but when a white man marries a black women
he got it going on
they look at him as someone with a strong enough sex drive to
have satisfied a black women, because black men are
suppose to be much larger then white men

or they look at him as if he is sleeping with his whore
his house keeper, or just another wench
in the back of their mind they look and admire, because they
want the same thing, but don't have the courage to put it on
front street
and the black man looks at her as if she is a sell out to her race

CHAPTER 25: PROVIDENCE

life isn't worth living unless you challenge it
I look at the older people who lived in the 50s and 60s and I see a different mentality
they seem to have different insight and hindsight about each other, and the treatment
that each other is giving
these are the people who had there floors scrubbed by the blacks and the Irish
yes the Irish people, the Irish was poor and had the reputation for drinking allot
in fact the Irish had such a bad reputation that they would be found drunk and laying on
the ground on the street corners that the police would have a special wagon to pick the
drunk Irish up off of the streets, the Irish was stereo typed and given the name paddy,
and that's how they came out with the name the paddy wagon
even to this day the police department still call their wagons I paddy wagons'
there was signs on buildings that read 'NO DOGS, NO NIGGERS< NO IRISH'
eventually times changed and this became an Irish country
the Kennedy's was Irish so why not a black president
separation and segregation goes back along ways and yes times have changed
but have they changed enough
when I was young I was a angry young man, i saw allot of injustice
i made allot of bad choices in life, I was a confused young man that blamed all of my
miss fortunes on the white man
yes most of my arguments was true, the white man has done allot of damage to the
black race
as we grow older, we grow wiser, and as we become wiser we began to take
responsibly for our own actions, and in so doing I realized that I have caused great harm
to myself as well
yes the game has been fixed, but it is my choice weather i want to play the game or not
for example, yeas the prison system is a form of slavery, but know one put that gun in
your hand, or that drug in your pocket but you, it was your choice to take that road
and yes you had a choice

I look at the young who was born in the 90s, and man I see the change, in personality
the change, in social behavior and in racial acceptance
the children of today have created a bond amongst each other that i have never seen
before
there was a time when we brought our children to the ball games
all races cheered for their team, we came together in sports and agreed on who was
the champ, or the best team we was pales in the bleaches
when the game was over we went our own separate ways, not ever even talking to
each other again
this generation are the people in the bleachers, giving more love and support for there

home team, they dress alike and listen to the same music, blacks and white friends
what does this say about our future
Martin Luther King JR had a dream, and his dream has come is coming true
the day is coming were we will not be judge by the color of our skin, but by the content
of our character

some people may say 'why keep looking into the past, let it go and move on with your
life, times have changed, it's not like it use to be?
if you are one of those people, well all i can say is, when did life get so good for you that
you forgot about the hard times and the people that are going through them
besides the past affects our future, what happened yesterday will always affect our
tomorrow
if what im saying is not true then how come we never forgot about the dream for a race
blind democracy
the times when we had to ride the color car on the train
how the separate but equal rights became the constitution which lead the democracy
when all schools shut down for the color students
when our economic and cultural needs was abused
how Sidney burshay and Louis Armstrong rose up with the gift of music and fought
segregation
and even though young black children didn't go to church together, but they all played
together on the same street
how the politicians in the 1960s built the high ways and by ways
ripping away the communities in the name of progress
the fight of integrating schools, desegregate
the 1980s drugs and gun fire

history teaches us and helps us to deal with our problems
it teaches us who we are where we are and where we come from
if we don't know where we came from, then we are without direction, to know where we
are going

here is a little bit of history for you if you believe that times have changed and things are
not like they used to be

one of the most powerful politicians of the united states was president
Thomas Jefferson
history would tell us that he was a great leader
a loving family man
history even gives him a name of high respect 'fore father'
one who ran this country as a true American an original patriot

he was the man who wrote that 'all men are created equal'
these are the facts

Thomas Jefferson was one who owned one hundred and 20 slaves
he lived in James town island in Virginia were they believed slavery began
from 1607 to 1612 there was a food drought
some solders starved to death, those that lived ate their own horses
some even liked up the blood of their fallen fellow solders
how did this happen? well when the Indians stopped trading war broke out
and the white English decided to take by force what they wanted at will
the Indians could only do so much with a bow and arrows
since they didn't have guns

the colonist had muskets and we know who had the upper hand in battle
by 1612 the drought was over
about that time the first Africans was brought over to work the tobacco fields
in 1770 a quarter of a million slaves worked in the James town colonies
they lived in small shacks on plantations 9 to in a small room
they worked from sun up to sun down
the life of a slave was a harsh one
slaves law was brutal the penalty for breaking the law was 30 lashes which cut so deep
that the most of the time the slave would die from the beatings or infection
or the law just consisted death for the slave
the sub floor pit was as whole under the floor were the slaves would hide their valuables
which was gun flint or cups and bowls, scissors and other small objects
they was just miss treated poor people who tried to make the best of their life
sound familiar ?

the house slave was of more value, they had never ending hours
slaves couldn't talk freely to white people
freed Negroes or skilled Negroes was sold off for about the same price
a winch was sold separately and most of the time they was separated from there
spouses and families
a slaves meal consisted of fish cornmeal or beans
the masters diet was pig, cow, and other fine cuts of meat
slaves ate very small portions with not enough nutrition to survive on, working from sun up
to sun down

THOMAS JEFFERSON, MARCHESELO AND FOUNDATION

Thomas got his marcheselo estate from his father
and that's where his 120 slaves lived and died

slaves was his livelihood and slavery was his industry
Thomas separated whites from blacks
he said that you couldn't free a slave
in fact he said it was like abandoning children
and yet he called his slaves family
he set his house up in such a design that you couldn't even see the slaves
yet he was still being served by them through hidden doors and secret hall ways, path ways and rooms
Thomas died in dept, the house was sold off and the slaves with it for they was nothing but property
Jefferson lived in a big house with allot of land, the slaves lived in ruins

why is the prison system full of mostly if not all black people?
what is the projects, ? or shall i dress up the word, low income housing
what is food stamps? a small portion?
what side of town do you live on? and can a black man be seen there?
do you take mass health?
divide and concur, prison, sold of into slavery
new laws, new laws, new laws why era they writhen and who are they writhen for?

the game is the same, the players are different, the strategy changed but the games the same

PRESIDENT ANDREW JACKSON

president Jackson a warier, a trooper an American soldier who has won many battles for his country

a orphan child who was a self made rich man loved by many

facts

Andrew Jackson owned over one hundred slaves
he also invaded Florida, used the slaves to fight for him or die
and stole land from the Indians, he was known as the Indian hater
in 1760s was Andrew Jackson, in 1775 was the revolutionary war
it was a constant threat of violence for the white man, even more for the slave
Andrew Jackson was known as a young trouble maker, with a bad gambling problem
he became a lawyer at the age of 20
he moved to the west because he had nothing going for him in the east
he moved east to start a new community
in 1788 three months before George Washington was president Jackson moved to

Tennessee
in the 1790s a women belonged to her husband like property
Jackson fell in love with a women named Rachel Donaldson who was already married
so they decided to elope to the south of the Mississippi river
Rachel's husband was so heartbroken and upset that he took the case to legislate
and won the case, it was the first divorce ever 'thanks to Jackson

in 1796 the state sent Jackson to congress as a state rep
back room deals and corruption stood in congress
after one year Jackson resigned, to race horses
Jackson loved fighting gambling and drinking
a man by the name of Charles Dickerson said something bad about Rachel
Jackson found out and challenged Charles to a gun fight
Jackson shot Charles and Charles shot Jackson in the chest
he lived and never got the bullet out
in 1812 the u-s declared war on the British
Jackson went to fight with his slaves on the front line and others from Tennessee
they traveled to the far east and ran into some Indians
after months in the woods with no food, some white solders tried to escape to go back
home, and Jackson had them executed

Jackson killed the crook warriors and took what he wanted when he wanted it
more native Americans was killed on horseshoe bend then any in American history
the battle in new Orleans was a victory that was spoken about for over one hundred
years
Jackson took his slaves to fight and defeated the British
8 killed with Jackson and hundreds of British was killed
the new American hero was Andrew Jackson
after 1850 America was free from Europe and its laws
it was called the Jackson era
Andrew became a wealthy man, from the strong hard working arms of the Negro slave
many poor white people came from Europe to live a better life off of the sweat of the
Negro slave
Jackson believed Negroes should be, and remain slaves
over one hundred slaves called him master
he made slaves believe he was there mother their father and there 'God'
slave grown products was the best product in the world
the money came from slave grown produce and the country and the slave owner got
rich
some of the bloodiest fights was in Georgia against the Indians
Jackson had a hate for free and escaped slaves

at first he was concerned about the Indians
then it was slaves and Indians, then just slaves
Jackson killed Negroes and Indians and he took over Florida

at this time in congress the voters did not choose the president of the u-s-a
the insiders in the white house and the big shots in Washington did
and the most unfit person to be chosen was Andrew Jackson
and even though Jackson did not qualify to be in office
in 1824 Andrew won the votes with the house reps
clay believed that Jackson should not be the president, so Adams became the president
John Quincy Adams and Henry Clay was accused of stealing the presidency

the revolutionary new style of voting came in 1820, when the public 'white' people was
able to vote and voice their opinion, and they voted Jackson in

a adulterer, murderer, hater, drunkenness slave master, became the president of the
united states
the campaign of 1828 was the dirtiest, underhanded campaign of all American history
it was the most disgraceful presidency that America would ever see
and yet you seek to find fault in the first black president
who ran a clean campaign 'why?'

yet we teach our children in history classes in our schools that these fore fathers was
great men
we should dear not speak against these men
as they sit there in class being addressed by the names that they took over from there
slave master, because the African slave had know identity
we are told that we are African American because we are Africans who was born in
America, yet the strong Indian features and ways that we have are not spoken of why?
no other nationality is address by the country of which there from first, then America
after, but the African Americans
the new breed, the dominate seed

foot note; as time continue to drift into the future
i see more inter racial relationships, marriages and children
there for one day whether you like it or not
•we will unite as one nation under God'

126

and god will be pleased
the African American people have been stripped
stripped from there way of life and living
striped from their culture and family tree
stripped from there God

see the Africans was to live the way that white America wanted them to, live my way or die my way
at one time it was nothing to walk pass a Negro hanging from a tree
or a head stuck on a pole
a pregnant women beaten to death
or a father mutilated and humiliated right in front of his children
times have changed they say, it's not like it used to be
i think of the sign that a man had hanging from his shoulders
it read a man was lynched today

then i think of the young black children in the court rooms
guilty, guilty for the color of their skin, or because of the neighborhood they live in
young black men, given 25, 30, even 60 years
for what? having a fire arm, something that they could have grown out of in a short time
given 25 years in the feds on a fIrSt offence, when a young white kid gets busted for drinking and driving
vehicular homicide, killed a whole family
and gets 2 to 4 years up state or maybe just probation depending on how much money he has or who he knows

a young black child is still trying to figure out, how to live the way that white America will except him
still trying to figure out, who they are, what they are, and were they came from
carrying the names of old president slave owners, Johnson, Thompson, Jackson, Washington ecL
young children living with the dream of being born with the privilege, as white people
to be labeled as someone, with some self worth, and self respect, as honest hard working productive people
and not treated less than, not to be looked down on, ' yet feared' and called names
so the young black man wears the sign around his shoulders for all to see, the way he walks, and talks and
express his self
he wants the world to read his sign, so he paints it black and gives it white lettering
the sign, the sign of the times, which reads 'I-AM-A-MAN
a man that lived, and died, and rose from the dead

a man with feelings and emotions, pride and honor, hopes and dreams
a man with strength and courage, mothers, fathers, and children
a man with the characters of God, with love and forgiveness
so once again, we can except you
we want unity, and equality, and peace for all mankind
we held on to GOD, and believed in change
and change we can

we are the back bone
we are the strength
we are the solders on the front line
we are the farmers and crop providers
we are family

WE ARE THE PRESIDENT
MADE IN AMERICA

I cannot finish this book without talking about our great deliverer
president Lincoln was we was taught that freed the slaves and became a hero by doing so
president Lincoln, the emancipation proclamation Mr. bicentennial himself
Lincoln freed the slaves that's what we are taught in our schools and most history books
we even have a memorial in Washington for his great achievements
Lincolns mother died when he was nine years old
in 1825 Lincoln died by a gunshot, he was buried in Springfield Illinois
there is also a museum in Springfield in his Homer
he was born in a cabin, he grew up poor
and now he is the most written about in American history
in 1859 he wrote the statement; the short a sable arums of the poor

the truth of Lincolns early life
he was a loyal honest man, with a good since of humor
he was a free thinker, who did not think likely of organized religion
a young lady by the name of Ann Rutledge was his only true love
she died at the age of twenty two, and that broke Lincolns heart
in fact it worried him so bad that he went into a deep depression
some even say that Lincoln had sex with prostitutes
Lincolns early life was a gloomy temperament
when Ann Rutledge died he was so depressed that his friends put him on what we would call
today suicide
watch
in 1841 he had another mental collapse, in 1867 he became a lawyer

it is believed that Lincolns battle with depression could have been his strength during the civil war

he has been the subject in over 1400 biographies

he had one term in congress in Washington, then he went on to practice being a lawyer

which most believe that helped his confidence

they say he educated his self

in 1841 he argued a defense for a black women slave from being a slave

then in 1847 he defended a slave owner to help him get his slaves back

Lincoln once said, if slavery was not wrong, then nothing is wrong

slavery became a prime subject in politics and by 1858 the argument was should they free the slaves or not

the two voices was from Lincoln and a man by the name of Steven Douglas

Lincoln and Douglas would debate about slavery all the time

Douglas once said that the declaration of independence did not apply to black people

Lincoln said it did, and that started allot of controversy

Steven Douglas tried to make Lincoln into a white republican

and to my surprise Lincoln was also a racist, yes you heard it correctly, Lincoln a racist

but the strange thing is, he also hated slavery

yet he was not a abolitionist

his main focus was to win his election

he as well as the average white man believed that white people was more superior then blacks

in 1963 Martin Luther king called Lincoln a light of hope in his speech in Washington

Malcolm X called Lincoln just another white man

we called him father Abraham the great emancipator

father Abraham once said 'blacks should never be able to vote nor run for office

in fact in 1858 he said that they should free all slaves and send them back Liberia were they came from

these are the factual statements of a man that we was taught that we should Homer as a hero

from 1820 to 1830 some of the greatest white people in history was here

those that helped with the underground rail road

from 1830 to 1850 Lincoln was silent, and he wouldn't give a voice nor lift a hand to help the slaves

so did he set the slaves free? or was he a politician pulled along by events ?

the fact is that Lincoln was a racist who sat on the fence about discussions

and we make him out to be a hero

he was what we call, three dimensional, with allot of racial views

don't judge president Lincoln from the 21st century, he was a 19th century man

in Feb. 1860 he left Illinois, and took a train to new York to convince the republican press that he can

compete on a eastern scale

so he gave a two hour speech that was printed in all the news papers across the country

he had to focus on his political image

a well known photographer named Brady helped him to become the president of the united states by

taking his pictures and sending them everywhere

all the news papers across the country

his pictures became so popular that people began to read about him everywhere

Lincoln ran his campaign, and defeated Douglas as well as his three other opponents

he wasn't even on the ballet in the south yet

he appointed all of his political rivals to be on his cabinet

I can pull up 43 presidents and talk about the mistreatment schemes and scams and politician games

if i was to do so, this book would be too big and expensive to perches

instead lets use the words of wisdom that president Clinton had to say

he said, and i quote ' 90 percent of life is how you respond to what happened to you not what happened'

so when i use the term 'we are the president'

WHAT ARE WE?

are we Lincolns, Jackson's, Johnson's, and Washington's

are we democrats, republicans and liberals

are we human beans, with feeling and emotions

are we created in the image of our creator

who is it God, or the devil

we are the most intelligent creature on this planet

created in the image of the most high

we are yet a mist of air, that is here and gone

what we do while we are here

will affect those of whom we leave behind, our history has proven that

there for today we are the future

in retrospect we have been given the power

and it is our responsibility

to take the mistakes from our pass, and make tomorrow a better day

for all

WE ARE THE PRESIDENT

maid in America

CHAPTER 26: PIMPS UP, WHORES DOWN

IF WE AS A PEOPLE, COULD EVER COME TOGETHER AS ONE, WHAT WOULD THIS WOULD BE LIKE

MOST PEOPLE YEARN FOR PEACE ON EARTH THROUGH RELIGION AND OTHER ORGANIZATIONS, THE OUT COME IS TO PUT BLAME ON THIS WOULD AND THE PEOPLE IN IT

WE LOOK FOR CHANG YET WE ARE NOT WILLING TO CHANGE, FOR CHANGE

A LOT OF US DON'T BELIEVE THAT WE CAN CHANGE THEREFORE THEY STAY STRONG TO BELIEVE THAT ONE DAY THE WHOLE WOULD IS GOING TO BE DESTROYED

No one is perfect, no one is righteous, we are all wrong doers, yet we spend our lives exulting our selves above others, miss judging and prejudging, for the most part we live in fear unable to admit it to ourselves nor our colleges that we are afraid

the unnatural thing is that we fear each other, when its God who we should be fearing

we have the tendency of living our lives constantly trying to meet some kind of financial status, and the higher we seem to climb, the less we look at those of whom we left behind, they don't seem to matter any more

the only time they are mentioned is when we are talking negative about them, not realizing that we can find ourselves in the same state that they are in

how hard is it to become hooked on drugs? or imprisoned? or to become a prostitute?

or even a murderer? a liar ? or just a small time thief

it could never happen to me, that's what is always said 'never say never
we used to say that we will never have a black president and now we do

_____never say never

This is a story about a dysfunctional family who over came some obstacles and struggle yet found it hard to beat the odds of addiction, that broke up there home and eventually took there lives

PIMPS UP, WHORES DOWN

Kim grew up in a small suburb town
she was fortunate enough to have both parents at home
her dad was a gynecologist and her mom was a engineer, so she grew up in a high
class community were most of her friends had no financial problems nether did her family
its Kim's last year in high school, and she is very excited to be the first one out of the
children in her immediate family to go to college
this is something she has been looking forward to for years, and now the time is finally coming
every so often when Kim is feeling down she would find herself going to the medicine
cabinet and finding one of her mother pills to take and make her feel better
Kim has been doing this for a little over a year with no side affects or problems
she was a popular girl in school, do to the fact that she was very attractive and dated
the star base ball player for a wile
on the day of her graduation she had a big party at her house, chaperoned by her mom
and dad, a lot of her family came from Florida, California, and Chicago from all over
she had a lot of support, there was one of her cousins from Chicago who invited her into
the bath room, she said she had something for her when they got into the bathroom they
locked the door, then Kim said 'what's up' her cousin pulled out a small bag with little
white rocks in it, and then she pulled out this glass stick and put one of the small white
peaces in a hole on top, then she took out a lighter and lit it, and smoked like she was
smoking a cigarette
her eyes got big and sweat started running down her forehead almost immediately
then she exhaled, and just sat on the toilet for a moment, then she handed the glass
stick to Kim, and with out thought Kim did the same thing her cousin did, when Kim
exhaled and looked at her cousin, she noticed her cousin on hands and knees on the
bath room floor looking for something and spacing out
so Kim asked her' what did you drop? her cousin said that she dropped a peace on the
floor, so there they was looking for a peace of rock on the floor, it was about 15 minutes
before Kim gave up, but she couldn't leave the bath room because she was bugging
and craving so bad, that she wanted more

about a hour went by and people started looking for Kim to open up her gifts and to cut
her cake
know one could find her, they looked every were except the bath room
until there was a knock on the bath room door, I guest some one had to use the bath
room, Kim wanted to say 'one minute' but couldn't get the words out of her mouth she
was so high

so her cousin said 'im going to be in here for a wile, some one said O.k. have you seen Kim? she said yes she is in here with me she is not feeling well

a couple of minutes went by .when Kim's mom came to the door

are you o.k. honey? yes i am fine mom. ill be out in a sec?

when Kim finally made it out she was high as a kite she couldn't function well

she was shacking and sweaty. and she thought that everyone may know what she did

so she went back into her moms stash to get a pill to come down .and she took it and it worked

she came back to her old self and the party went on with a happy ending

for the next couple of weeks. Kim focused on packing for college. and moving on with her life

her first day at school went pretty good, she had a real nice dorm and her room mate

was a girt friend from her old school, so they got along well

the next day they stepped out on the college grounds

they noticed very few people was socializing. it wasn't as happy and go lucky as her old school

she said i guest the students here have there education on there mind, and just kept on with her day

her room mate suggested to go out that night .so that was there plan to go out and mangle

A NIGHT ON THE TOWN

so there they were. looking for some action from one store to another

for the most part they was just window shopping

when they noticed a small dinner and they went in

it was a small elegant place with a night club in the rear. playing loud music

so they decided not to eat until later •they went dancing and had one heck of a good time

the next day they went with there daily classes .Kim over heard two girls talking about the same club she was at last night

one girt said them ignorant niggers are always stirring up trouble. they just cant do nothing in peace. it was a simple transaction. all he had to do was take the money

it was such a shark to Kim because these girls were white just like Kim. and she couldn't understand because last night there was white and black people in the club and every one seemed to be getting along

the next week they went back to the same club. instead of Friday it was Saturday and the same music was being played when they entered

so there they were in the club ordering drinks and chatting

133

when Kim noticed that they was the only white people in the club
that's when this young well dressed man approached them in a friendly kind of way
so were you all from he said? Kim told him about going to school and they hit it off with
a good conversation
the young mans name was little, Kim asked him why do they call you little. your not
little? he replied. they call me little because i don't ask for much. just a little
they danced and exchanged phone numbers and
he was such a well dress nice gentlemen, he even drove them back to school in his nice
bens

the next day Kim just couldn't get him off of her mind, so she called him
when she called him he didn't recognize who she was at first until she refreshed his
memory
they talked for a wile, and he asked her out on a date, she said o.k. and hung up the
phone
she was so happy .she called home and told her parents, mom and dad was so happy
for her until they found out that he was black
then they was totally against the date and relationship
her parents said that she did not go to college to date, but to work on her currier
Kim was so up set because her parents always told her that people are people and that
race didn't count
she wasn't razed to hate anyone because of there race
so her and her parents go into a big fight, then Kim just hung the phone up
and went on the date any ways
when little got to the school to pick Kim up, he was such a gentlemen he even opened
the back door for her
when Kim was getting into the car she realized it was the back door, then she
understood why
there was two women already in the car, the one in the front was a little older then the
one in the back seat. they seem to be nice people
they had nice hair and clothes, Kim didn't say nothing at first until the girls introduced
them selves
the one in the front said hello first her name was Monica, the one in the back was
named pat

so they struck up a conversation and was having a enjoying time until Monica
pulled out a crack pipe and started passing it around
every one took a hit off of the pipe but Kim, so Monica decided to pass it to Kim
it all came back to Kim's memory, the incident at her graduation party
Monica asked her 'have you ever got high before? Kim said yes
then Monica asked her if she liked it, Kim said yes but i, before she can get another word

out of her mouth Monica yelled' then what the fuck is the problem now, you think your
to good for us black niggers, miss prissy college girl
Kim said know that's not it, little tell her im not like that?
little said I don't know what your like, 0111 know is that you don't want to party with us
Kim felt out numbered riding in a car with strangers, and with the fight she just had with
her parents she needed a drink, a pill, or something so she said o.k. ill take a hit
and started drinking and smoking up a storm

KIM'S NEW CAREER

odd of a sudden the car stopped and every one got out
Kim was so high she couldn't talk to ask were they was going
when they got out and started heading for this apartment house, little took a key out
and opened the door
Kim was thankful that his apartment was on the first floor, because she couldn't make it
up know stairs
when they got inside, the house was clean but quiet and dark
the two girls sat down on the couch, and little went into another room
Kim just stood there waiting for someone to tell her to sit down, know body did
so she stood there until little yelled for her to go into the room he went into
she went in to find little undressed and laying on the bed
the first thing he did was offered her another hit, she took it and he continued to give her
more and more, she was so high that that's all she wanted was another hit
then she noticed that he stopped giving her a hit so she asked him for one
that's when he said 'what you going to do for me?
she said what do you mean? he said take your clothes off and get into bed with me? she
said know i don't want to?
he said you owe me for all that coke i just smocked with you, now how you going to pay
me back, what you thought this chit was free, it cost me a lot of fucking money
she said please can i have another hit, she was so high that that's was on her mind
he said again 'what you going do for me?
she said ill do anything you want just give me another hit please?
he said not until you take off all of your clothes and get into bed with me?
she did everything he wanted including oral sex, and that's were she spent the night
the next morning she was getting her stuff together to leave, she felt so bad for how she
was acting that she started to apologize to Monica and pat
they said you don't owe us no fucking apology, and ant nothing to be ashamed about
girl, you are a trooper i like that, you wanted something and you did what you had to, to
get it, i like you your classy
then Monica and pat sat her down and explained to her that she can get high every
night
if she wanted to, Kim said know, that she didn't want to get high know more

she asked pat if she can wake little up, so he can take her back to her dorm
pat said yah sure ill wake him up, then she went into the room to get him
when she came out she said he is in the shower, he said wait a moment
then she started walking toward Kim with a smoking crack pipe in her hands
then she passed it to Kim, and Kim was back at it, like a dog to a bone
this time they wasn't as generous, that's when they told Kim that they was working girls
and that if she would hang out with them that they can put a lot of money into her
pockets, and if she wants some more crack that she world have to join the team
Kim was so high and out of it that she agreed, and forgot all about going back to her
dorm

they was in Kim's head for hours, just drilling her and schooling her on how to turn a trick
what to look out for, and how much fun they could be having partying and getting high
all the time, each time they felt Kim being doubtful they gave her another hit

LIFE ON THE STREET

when the sun went down they all got into the car and headed out
first they dropped pat off on a busy comer
then Monica and Kim got dropped off at another corner
as soon as they got out of the car Monica took Kim down a alley way and gave her a hit,
then Monica said after you turn your first trick ill give you more
the corner was full of life, the city life, lights and action
a small car pulled up and Monica started talking to some man and then she called Kim
when Kim came over Monica said your up, as soon as Monica got into the car the man
said so what's your name? Kim said my name is Kim, do you think you can drop me off
at the college campus? the man said sure when we are don ill take you were you want
to go
so they parked and Kim did everything she was instructed to do, when she was done
she asked the man to take her to the college campus and he said, sorry i was instructed
to bring you right back
besides i don't think little would appreciate me not taking you back to him?
she said you know little? he said yes i do he sent me to test you and baby you failed
the man dropped Kim over little house, little came down stairs and told her to go up
stairs
then he got the report from the man and went up stairs and started slapping Kim around
and calling her all kind of selfish bitches
he took his belt off and beat her like she was a child, she sat there in tears
then little came back out of the room with some more crack and gave it to Kim
then he sat next to her and started talking to her
he said that he would take care of her, and that he loved her and didn't want anything
to happen to her, then he made her a sandwich and said ill make sure you eat dress and

feel good, then they had a drink and he gave her a small amount of crack, just enough
to make her want for more
then they got back into the car, and he dropped her back on the corner
Monica and pat was there, they was very upset at Kim
Monica told pat that Kim left her out on the street by her self
and they both threatened to kick Kim's ass if she ever did that bullshit again
the next few tricks Kim turned and came back, each time she did little would give her a
little crack, like giving a dog a treat after he did a trick

at the end of the night every one ended up at little house
little came into the room and pat and Monica gave him all of there money
then every one looked at Kim, Kim gave him her money, then little gave each of the girls
ten dollars, Kim said after all of the work we did this is all your going to give us
fuck you, you ungrateful bitch, who's going to pay rent, and car insurance, or bail your
punk ass out when you need it
little now you know why they call me little. because all your ever going to get from me
bitch is a little?
he said last night you smoked up over a thousand dollars worth of chit?
until you pay me back that's all your going to get? then he gave her a little more crack
they sat there smoking and drinking until the sun up

THE GREAT ESCAPE

Kim missed weeks of school and was behind on her work, her family constantly tried to
get in touch with her with no success
her mom and dad was not getting along, they was fighting a lot and taking there stress
out on each other, patiently waiting for the police to contact them in regards of there
missing daughter
there was a lot of talk going around that Kim's mom started to drink her problems away
and when she did she became this violent out of control person
Kim's dad was in therapy and was trying to get her mom into some kind of ala program
Kim's mom would not go to therapy, because she blamed Kim's disappearing on him
so the family became very dysfunctional

as for Kim she was still doing her thing with little Monica and pat
Kim was part of the team now and she was working longer and longer hours
not just at night but also in the day, every day even Sunday
she began to loose wait and look poorly
it was the first of the month on a Friday night, the streets were jumping with dealers and
tricks, hustlers from all walks of life
little was surprised at Kim's achievements, she became this fast talking con artist
she got so good at the game, she was able to turn a trick, pick his pockets, and even

though he knew she was picking his pockets he didn't care, because she was making him feel so good, and before he could complain she was gone

so there she was putting in work when this man that she never saw before drove up to her, wearing a smile and flashing a hand full of cash

she did the same thing she always did, walked with a slow sexy tone and grabbed his attention

he ask her was she a working girl? she said, do you want to party?

he said get into the car, so she did, they drove about a half of a block when the man pulled over and showed her a police badge and started reading her wrights

suddenly Kim just looked at the cop, and said your not a cop let me out of this fucking car, my people know were im at and who im with, don't think you can get away with this

at first she thought it was some one trying to rap her, until she saw that the badge was real

the man put the hand cuffs on Kim and took her to the police station

wile in the station they started to question Kim, who's your pimp?

were do you Jive? what's your name? who do you get your drugs from?

how long have you been doing drugs?

Kim didn't tell the police nothing, she was smart enough to know the un writhen rules of the streets I don't snitch

she also gave an alias name, but when they ran her finger prints they found out who she really was

when the police ran her record they was surprised that she had know record

then when they found out were she was from and that she was in the system as a missing person they contacted her parents

when her parents came to pick her up, they were sharked at what she was arrested for and in denial about the whole ordeal

they told the police that she called the house and was seeing this black man

and that's the last time they herd from her

they told the police that the black man kidnapped her and was asking them for money but they didn't know were Kim was

the story had to many loop holes, so they investigated and once again

the police questioned Kim and Kim denied everything

so they bailed Kim out and took her home

A NEW BEGINNING

once Kim got home she felt so ashamed for the choices she has made that was ruining her life

so she sat down with her parents and told them some of things that she was going through

she left out the drug addiction and prostitution, she said that the police was mistaken

because of the people she was hanging out with had a bad reputation
she lied and blamed everything on Monica and pat. she also said that little was a good
man, and that he had nothing to do with her friends or her being missing
she remained at home for a week, and then her dad spoke with the dean and got her
back into school
she was doing good in school, and stayed away from calling little for two months
she found herself having these dreams about drugs .that kept getting stronger and
stronger until she just caved in and called little
hi little how have you been?
little   im o.k. were have you been?
Kim,   i am bake in school and doing fine?
Kim,   i will like to see you
little   ill be right over to pick you up
when little arrived he saw Kim with looking healthy and clean, she even spoke differently
she sounded like her old self again
so they sat and talked for a wile, and then Kim just came out and asked him for a hit
he said lets go to my house
this time Kim was watching the directions, so if she needed to she could find her own
way back to school
Kim said i just want to do one to get this monkey off of my back
little said yah! me to
and they started to get high, before Kim knew it she was there for two days and she was
back on the streets hustling
on the third day she just went back to school and got her self together
she started going to n/a meetings and meeting a lot of nice people in the n/a program
she had some real friends who she can speak openly with, people who understood her
and most of the girls was ex working girls like herself and she loved it
the year was over and she went home for spring break
this time when she went home she found her mom drinking really bad
her dad was not living at home know longer, he moved in with another women and was
divorcing her mom

the house was up for sale and her mom lost her job
the worst thing was when Kim found out that she was pregnant she wasn't sure who the
father was, sometimes she used protection and sometimes she didn't
but for the most part, the chances that it could have been little was high
she became very distraught and confused
she didn't want an abortion, and she didn't want a child to stop her from completing
school
she didn't know how to tell her parents, and she really didn't know how to tell little
having him in her life at this time was bad, it jeopardized her recovery

so she went to her meeting and talked about it

after the meeting she was approached by several friends who gave her several different types of advice

so for the first time in years she got down on her knees and prayed

she prayed until tears started running down her eyes

wile she was in her room praying her mother walked into the room, and said i don't know why your praying it don't work look what God has done for me?

at that point Kim jumped up and said who the hell do you think you are to say some bull shit like that, after all we are going through as a family i would think you would be praying to God to at leased get dad back?

her mother said i don't need know man in my life for nothing i don't have know little children to raise all i have is my self?

that's when Kim said i do have a child in my stomach and its by little, and im going to need his help to help me raise my child, so please bring me to him so i can tell him that he is going to be a father?

her mother was furies, she blew up screaming and yelling, im going to tell your father you little selfish slut, after all the hard work we have done to get you into school so you don't turn out to be a know body, you turn around and get pregnant by a know body, is this the way you repay us

her mom got on the phone and called her dad, he came right over

the first thing he said was, i have a friend who can give you an abortion know questions asked?

Kim said know, i am keeping my baby

her father said, if you keep that child don't you ever talk to me again young lady

her mother stood up and looked her right into the eyes and said

i love you very much, and i understand what you are going through, but you really have to think this through

and if this is what you want well, then so be it

ill be by your side and i will help you as much as i can, that's what family is fore

her dad then stomped out of the house and left

the next day her mom took her to visit little

when they got to the house little was not home so Kim called him

and told him that she had something very important to tell him

he said he had something to tell her too

when he arrived he was walking, Kim said were is your car?

he said its in the impound and he need to get it out today

he said he needed Kim to put some work in to help him get his car out

Kim knew that little had a gambling problem and the first thing she thought was that he might have lost it gambling again

so she said what do you have to tell me?
ha said Monica found out that she has aids and she is not taking it very well
and pat was found dead in the back of a old boarded up building
Kim started to cry, and said that could have been me
then Monica walked in the door, with her head down and she started crying too
then her and Kim hugged each other in tears
Monica said i got my people looking into it, we are going to find out who did this to pat
Kim said my mom is in the car, i have to leave
then little asked Kim not to leave because he needs her to be here for him 'now'
then Kim said i cant
little said after all i have done for you, you cant
she said know
he said why?
she said im pregnant with your child
he said well that don't matter, after the abortion you will feel better
she said im keeping my baby
he said how do you know that its my baby?
she said its your
then he jumped up and pulled her hair, and said you bitch you are going to stay here
and put this fucking work in, tell your mother to leave ill take you home
she said know
then he took his fist and punched her dead in the middle of her stomach
she stooped over in great pain and started to cry
then he pulled her up and told her he was sorry and that he loved her
and when this is all over that he was going to straiten up and they will be a family
he then got on one knee and asked Kim to be his wife
she said yes then he told Monica to go out side and to tell her mother that he was giving
her a ride home
her mother left, and then he took Kim into his room and offered her some crack
she said know not wile she is pregnant
then Monica said its O.k. girl i smoked my whole pregnancy, with all of my children it
wont harm them
Kim took a hit and once again she was off and running
unable to come to her senses, she just kept on going
this was her longest run yet
she told little that she just dint care know more
her life has been shattered and all of her dreams was just taken away from her
in a puff of smoke
she moved in with little, and never went back to school
she recruited several working girl for little, and the house was wide open in full flight
little didn't spend much time at home, and Kim was nine months pregnant

she worked up until her eighth month, then she just found it hard to walk the streets
she would always complain about her feet, or her appetite, it just became so noticeable
that she was pregnant that little took her off of the streets

LIFE AND DEATH

it was three a clock in the morning, little was up smocking with a few of his working girls
Kim was right there smoking, she kept feeling labor pains but she didn't say nothing to
know one, she was afraid that they may call the ambulance and she wont be able to
keep smocking
it was all good until she looked down between her legs and saw a puddle of water
then she jumped up and yelled '0 shit my fucking water just broke'
to her surprise know body moved, every one was stuck
a couple of seconds went by before anyone realized what was happening
little told every one to put everything away, clean the house and lets go
we got to go to the hospital, Monica called the hospital before hand
and told them that they was on the way
she wanted little to call a ambulance but he said hell know
don't you know if we call a ambulance that the police will come with them?
im dirty like a mother fucker, i ant trying to get locked on the night my baby is born

so there they was at the hospital, little told Monica to stay with Kim wile he hit the block
a few hours went by and little didn't return yet, Monica got worried and called him
he didn't pick up, so Monica went up stairs to Kim's room
the first thing Kim said when she saw Monica was were is little?
Monica said i don't know, he said he was going out to check the block
Kim said that's fucked up, take this number and tell my mom im here
when Monica called Kim's mom, she was drunk and talking crazy
she said who is this? its Monica, Kim's having the baby im at the hospital with her, and
she asked me to call you
Kim's mom said i ant going know were
she deserves all the pain and miss fortune that is coming her way
i told her about hanging with you ungrateful low life black niggers
you ruined her, she was a good girl until she mix up with you people
wile she was on the phone with her mom little walked into the room
he told Monica to hang the phone up and get out of the room
the doctor came and they started to prepare Kim for the delivery

there they was in the hospital room Kim was pushing the child out, and little was holding
her hand
push, push, little was excited, his first boy
he had a lot of dreams for his son, he felt so good he called his mother

and that was strange for him to do, he never introduced his mother to none of his
whores
finally the head was coming out slowly, the doctor was slowly pulling the babies
head so little really couldn't see the baby at first, but when he did he yelled out real loud
what the fuck is this?
doctor, doctor what is going on, look at me im dark with brown eyes, this baby has blond
hair and funny colored eyes
this ant my mother fucking baby
as he ran out of the hospital he passed Kim's mom, he was so pissed off that he just
looked at her, and shook his head

little went home and got drunk, and passed out on the couch
about three in the morning hi whores showed up with his money and they continued to
get high
little was telling the story about his experience at the hospital like he was still pissed off
when odd of a sudden the door was kicked in and in seconds his house was full of police
they arrested everyone in the apartment including little
they read him his rights and took him into the police station, little said give me my phone
call ill be out before sunup
wile at the station they questioned every one but little, two hours or so went by then they
took little into a small room and started to question him about murder charges and they
also added white slavery
they pinned pats death on him and locked him up with know bail
little sat in the county jail for six months before going to trial
that morning in the court room a lawyer that the courts gave him approached him and
tried to convince him to plead out to man slaughter charges, and his sentence can be
reduced to 15 to 20, if not he can do life on a first degree
little said i never told you i was guilty why do you want me to cop a plea
ill get my own lawyer get away from me, when little interred the court room
he saw all of his whores sitting with the public and talking with the district attorney's
he stood up and looked at them all and said what the fuck is going on
they couldn't even look at him, they just sat there with there heads down
then the court officer yelled all rise, and the judge came out
the judge read the charges and then looked at little and read the charges to him
drugs possession, school zone, white slavery, and murder
when little herd the charges he almost fainted, the court officers had to hold him up for
a second
everyone took the stand against him, even his number one whore Monica
when Monica got on the stand she was shedding tears and talking real slow, like some
one had a gun in her back and making her talk
that's when little knew that the 'd' boys had her in the grip, and the odds was against her

so she was playing her best hand

then after she confessed to everything, she said to the judge 'your honor every one is testifying to save there own butts, some off us have been couched and forced to take this stand and turn untrue evidence over

there fore most claims are unreliable informant information, how can this be used as evidence against the defendant

that information called for a miss trial, and once again Monica saved the day

eventually little got off on technicalities, they had know search warrant when they kicked in the door the apartment, and as for pat and the murder charges there was know sufficient evidence that little murdered her

after waiting for trial for three years he finally got off

back on the street starting from square one with nothing

the word on the streets was that Monica and Kim was doing real swell

so little went looking for them, but couldn't find them know were

then he put the word on the streets that he was looking for them

he had to find them because he had know place to lay his head

so he did what he was trying not to do, he called Kim's moms house

the phone just ring and went to the answering machine, he hesitated to leave a message

but when he did all he said was, this is little tell Kim to come see me

then he hung the phone up and thought, were the hell is she going to see me at

the only place she knew to meet me at was my old house

so he took the train to his old house

when he got on the street he looked and said 'dam' that bens is just like the one i use to have

he thought it was a funny that the same kind of car he had was sitting in front of his old place

he went and sat on the steps looking around and reminiscing about the old days

when the front door opened, and there standing before him was Monica Kim and a little boy about three years old

the girls jumped for joy, hugging and crying, little almost cried but held his tears back

Kim then call the little boy L-L come meet your daddy

little didn't know how to respond, the child that he denied looks just like him, except for his complexion, other then that he was little all over again

they went back up stairs and began to school little on what's been going on wile he was away

Kim's mom cleaned her life up and got custody of L-L, Kim said right after he was born child care came and took him because cocaine was found in his system

she said her mom stepped to the plate like a real trooper, and because she did that im able to spend time with our son

the other whores that was trying to send him away got what they had coming

as you can see me and Monica been holding it down for you we never gave up
your car is out side, you suits are in the closet and we want you back on top of your
game
little was down for it all, he said the pimp game is in my blood
my dad was a pimp and his dad was a pimp, he said he was born pimping, but he did
not want his son to be one
little said i ant been high for three years, i don't even smoke cigarettes know more
so for now on we goanna handle our business the right way
we goanna bye a house so we can leave something to our son if anything was to
happen to us, at lease he will have something to fall back on
so business went on, little stopped working the streets, he had clients meet his whores at
the crib and money was flowing
three weeks went by and little was unpacking some of his old clothes, when he found a
jacket that he used to we're when he dressed down
so he checked the pockets and found a small bag of crack, when he saw it old feelings
just took him and with out to much thought ha started getting high
that night when the girls came in, little was high as a kite
they asked him what he was doing and he told them 'hay i never had a party for being
home so lets just have one for tonight only, and then tomorrow we will stop
o.k. Monica said but Kim was against it, little gave Kim a drink and got into her ear until
she join the party
two weeks went by and Monica was not looking good. so little took her to the doctor's
the doctor told her that if she didn't stop using drugs that she would die soon
they tested her blood and it wasn't looking to good, Monica tried to stay clean but she
just could not stop using do to the fact that she was still around little and Kim and they
was smocking every chance they got
Kim got a good score one Friday night wile turning a trick, she picked his pocket and
came out with over three thousand dollars
little sat some money aside for L-L he was going to take him shopping the next day
and rent was do so he put some aside for rent, then he got some crack and started
dealing
he sat Kim and Monica down and told them that he was switching his game up
he was dealing crack and he wants them to bring him some costumers
so they hit the streets and was bringing crazy business to little
little still made them work and at the same time they was dealing and smoking

one Saturday after a long weekend, Kim and little went to pick up L-L from Kim's moms
house
they took him shopping and it was all good until they got home, they walked into the
house and noticed the door wasn't locked little ran into his room were he kept his stash
and his stash wasn't there, so they got into the car and took L-L home

145

then they hit the block looking for Monica
they was putting the word out that they was looking for her and couldn't find her know were
little called his connect, reed up and went home and went back to business
the next morning one of there costumers called and said i need to see you man
little said what's up
he said i got some info for you, but you got to give me a wake up
im on 'e' and i got to get off
O.k. little said come over
when he got there he told little that Monica was found dead in this base hotel, she was in the praying position with a crack pipe in her hand

little just put his head down and started crying like a baby
Kim looked at him strange because she never saw little break down like that for know one
little shut down shop and took Kim to go and identify the body, and it was her dead as a doornail
Monica three children in Boston some were, little said know family has been in her life for the last 14 some years he's known her .
then he looked at Kim and said, we the only family she got
so little handled the funeral arrangements, he found some of her old letters that she wrote wile she was in prison
and he contacted every one she wrote to, the sad thing was the wake and the funeral was on the same day
the only ones that showed up was little, Kim, Kim's mom and L-L, out of all the people she's known that claimed they loved her just 4 people at her funeral
little took that personal, his heart grew hard and he stopped giving people breaks
if you didn't have strait money you wasn't getting nothing

time went on and little wasn't letting Kim work know more
he put her right down with him in the drug game and they was blowing up
the only problem was that they was there own best costumers, they wasn't saving know money, all of there profits went up in smoke
they found there selves living with Kim's mom for a wile, and then they applied for low income housing just to find there selves living in the projects
L-L is sixteen now and he visits almost every day
little finally put his foot down and decided to drinking and drugging
he felt as though it was time to start raising his family
he said he was tied of going to jail and watching people he cared about die
he realized that he wasn't getting ahead especially after he lost his car, and his crib
he found himself out of character, and doing things to himself and his family that he

really didn't want to do

besides, Kim is pregnant again and little has made dramatic changes in his life

they both go to n/a meetings together and has been clean for two years

Kim's mom goes to a/a meetings and they talk recovery all the time

Kim is going back to school, and little picked up a construction job with one of his buddies from the program

little talks to L-L all the time about his life, and his father and grand dad

he told L-L about the streets and the people in it, the pimp game and why he should not be one

he told little what his dad told him, that the first pimps was slave masters who sold winches for sex

and he believes that's were his grand dad may have learned it from

he believed that his grand dad was looking for work and couldn't find any

and being the good looking big strong block man he was, had many women who needed his protection approached him, because white men was roping and taking advantage of block women so much, that a block Negro women couldn't even get a job cleaning house unless they were putting out to the man

he was schooling little about the prose and cons in life

it broke little's heart when L-L quit high school

L-L grew up ruff, he watched his dad pimp his mom, and watched them both using drugs, fighting over drugs

and he sow his dad cheat on his mom, life was a mess for that young boy

he never got to know his grand father, because he ran off when he found out his mom was pregnant by a block man, and his grand mother stayed drunk

now every one is claiming to be clean, and trying to school L-L to stay on the right path

LITTLE/LITTLE, GETTING BIG

but L-L was thinking differently

he felt as though he was his own man with his own life

he loved his parents but had very little respect for them L-L grew up very angry, angry at the would, for the life he had to live, and he blamed every one for his misfortunes

L-L was named L-L after his dad, he was really a Jr, they called him l-L short for little, little

L-L started hanging with gong members and drug dealers at a young age

he looked up to the thugs in the projects, with there nice clothes and nice cars

L-L was a chip off of the old block, he was just like his dad

he liked to dress nice and he would dream of getting a nice car one day

all the girls in the project thought he was fine because he had block features

witch he got from his dad, and strait hair which he got from him mom

only very few knew he had a white mom, he sort of tried to hide that do to the fact that

a lot of people in the projects spoke bad about white people most people mistaken him for being Spanish and he didn't core

so all excepted him, the older players on the street schooled the younger ones

about little SR, and put him on such a pedestal that even the younger thugs gave L-L his props

at the age of seventeen L-L was in full affect with his hustle, he was a small time crock dealer and most thought of him as a player

it seemed as if every time you sow him he was with another girl

he dressed sharp and didn't toke know shorts from know one, even those who was older then him, he didn't core who you was if he felt as though you disrespected him he would get you

one day little sr and Kim was coming home after a AA meeting

as they was driving down the main street, they sow the police putting l-L into the bock of the police car

Kim jumped out of the car to ask the police what was they arresting her son for

she jumped out so fast and ran up to the police that before little could stop her the police just opened fire and shot her

Kim was laying in a puddle of blood and L-L was in the back of the police car witnessing it all, unable to do anything about it

little just sat there in a daze, unable to believe any of this was happening

Kim was seven months pregnant and there she was shot in cold blood in the middle of the main street, by a police officer who was just in training

as he watched his son in the back of a police car getting driven away from his mothers dead body all he could do was sit in shark

about three police men surrounded the car and yelled, freeze show me your hands

as if they wanted him to have a weapon or something so they can justify the shooting

they laid him on the ground and cuffed him

took him to the station and charged him with interfering with an arrest

so there they sat L-L and little in grief over the death of Kim

L-L was being charged with a hand to hand drug charge, and he had a five hundred dollar bail

little got out on a personal, and he came back and bailed L-L out, and they went strait to the hospital morgue to check on Kim, who was pronounced D-O-A

it was a sad situation, all of Kim's family came to the house, every one seemed to be in tears even the friends from the n/a and a/a program

Kim had a lot of people who loved her, even her father showed up for a short time

he wanted to stay but Kim's mom wasn't happy with him at all

know one saw him after that he didn't even show up to the funeral

the funeral was nice they did a good job on Kim's body, little was so broken up he didn't know if he was going left or right

family and friends tried to talk with him but he wasn't talking to know one
it was as if he snapped or something, the police that shot her was suspended with pay
and the news papers got a hold of the news and printed the whole thing on the front
page
they made it seem like it was Kim's fault and they really said some bad things about L-L
they called him a local drug dealer, with a father with lengthy record, they made it
seem like Kim was still working the streets by calling her a well known prostitute
little was so pissed off the first thing came to his mind was, im going to get that cop
for killing my wife, and he meant it

after the funeral little bailey went out, and he stopped going to meetings all together
L-L was doing 18 months in the county jail for drug possession with the intent to sell
wile in prison L-L was labeled a gang member because of a tattoo he had on his
shoulder which read Little, Little it was only his name but the administration still labeled
him S-T-G a member of a street gang, which put him on 23 hour lock down because of
his status
he had complete a program and denounce his affiliation to get off of gang status
finally he made it to general population, on his first day out he had problems with the
other inmates because he looked like this young square kid that didn't fit in
he didn't fit in with the white inmates or the black, the Spanish almost adopted him until
they realized that he wasn't Spanish, so for the most part he found himself by him self
some black dudes tried to make fun of him at times, by calling him a half bread, or
zebra boy, but there was Muslim brother who spoke up her L-L and told them boys that L-L
was
black, because black is the dominate seed, know matter what you mix it with its
still black, cant you see the color of his skin
he told them boys that they may have people in there own family lighter then L-L
so those boys cooled it, and left L-L alone

one day wile walking the yard another inmate tested him by coming at him with some
sexual homosexual type stuff, L-L took a pin out of his pocket that had a razor melted
into it and cut that boy up real bad
when the other inmates saw that L-L was a stand up guy they started giving him respect
after a couple of months L-L met some older cats that knew his father
and they put him under there wings, and L-Ls bid became easier

little slowly went back to his old ways
he just couldn't deal with living with out Kim, and with out the program he just started
dealing and using again
one night Little went to meet his connect when some dudes tried to jack him for his
money

Little stepped back to try and get a look at there faces, when he realized he knew them
he said are you for real man, then he reached for his gun
before he can get to it, the man pulled out a knife and began to stab little repeatedly

L-L was sitting in his jail sell when he got a letter from his grandmother telling him that
his dad was stabbed to death, in a drug transaction gone bad
L-L went to school wile in the joint
he got out and turned his life around
he became a drug counselor for those a risk
he also started his own youth program against gangs, drugs, and violence
he became a mentor in his community
parents would bring there troubled children so L-L can lecture and counsel them
some young thugs from the passed kept pushing up on L-L
some one remembered him from the projects he use to live in
apparently is was a rival gang who still had some grudges
L-L tried to explain to these cats that he wasn't down with know gang or gang activity
and every time he saw then they would give him these hard looks, wile throwing up the
signs
L-L knew the reality on the streets and he wasn't taken know chances with his life
so he tried to stay as fare away from them boys as possible
L-L grew up in a projects that they called Richmond street
and these was some east side boys from stillman ave, and he knew that stillman ave
wasn't know joke
but in order for him to get to hill street projects were he worked
he had to pass through stillman ave, and he was on parole and he had a lot to loose
so he would take the long way around crescent street, even in the middle of the winter
in bellow zero weather, to stay out of harms way

he was walking down the street and got shot, in the middle of a cross fire
the bullet wasn't meant for him, or was it
he died a hero, a living example of 'change we can'
this is one of the poems he used in his work shops when teaching the youth
to live in peace

behaviors passed down through generations
who do we blame. for these situations
as we look to heaven. we live a lie
know body knows were we go .when we die
if there is a heavenly home
and its not just a dream
i want to talk. to Martin Luther king

and let him know his dream came true
shown with the peace and love
that lies within 'you'

so lets live in peace and unity
and be what we are meant to be
I know to those, that judge us it sounds strange
that a pimp. a hustler .a whore .can change
a old wise man use to say
we all must meet our maker one day
the question rises as the trumpet sounds
do pimps stay up, and whores stay down
change your way of thinking .my friend
or death will be your tragic end

keep dreaming of a place .were we all can relate
know death .know pain. and know more hate
know wars .know hunger. and know more greed
were living in hominy, is truly guaranteed
know • crimes .know jails, or institutions
and know more racist pollution
then we will know we are heaven sent
and we wont need no president
until that day of refuge come
be thankful for all of us. haven one
one alone is irreverent
for if we become one
we become one. 'president'

**WE ARE THE PRESIDENT
MAID IN AMERICA**

CHAPTER 27: LET ME BE

LET ME BE 'ME'

what will I be)f you just let me be ?
would I be a man of integrity
a house nigger
would you would be my responsibility

a field nigger
praying to be, 'free'
a doctor performing open heart surgery
or just another black bastard in a ran down community

tell me, what will I be?

WHAT I BE IF YOU LET ME BE?

would we have a better history
would I be a king or a chief
with my own tribal religious beliefs
would I be oppressed or depressed
thought of as less, in a world that wont let me rest

you didn't see the sign of God
a slave out living three masters
working sun up, to sun down
jumping highest, running the fastest

WHAT WILL I BE, ' IF YOU LET ME BE I'

would I be alive
or will I be dead
because once again I listened to the lies you said
that I am not a man
that I am less than
that I am African American
that I will never understand
the ways of the land, that was stolen from the Indian

WHAT WILL I BE, IF YOU LET ME BE ?

would I be a jail bird
not welcome in society
would I be a statistic living in poverty
would I be a low life
would I be a peasant
would I be a leader
would I be president

WHAT WILL I BE IF YOU LET ME BE ?

ILL BE FREE,
TO BE
WHAT GOD HAS INTENDED ME, TO BE 'ILL BE ME'

CHAPTER 28: SOME MUST DIE

THEREFORE SOME MUST DIE

I can only imagine
the emotions people who were mad about
The burning of synagogues
Some were afraid some were sad
but I can only imagine that some was mad.

I would have been confused
because we would never understand why
People put themselves above others
so high that others would have to die

The Germans invaded Poland and imposed
restrictions on the Jews
put them in the ghetto
with nothing to lose from concentration camps

To exterminate a race
I can only imagine the look on another's face
To be separated from her husband
and watch her children die
because the German believed

The hateful, selfish, unlawful lie
that all people are not created equal
Therefore some must die

A COTTON PICKING SHAME

Through blood, sweat and tears
Oppressed for four hundred and thirty five years
We all need somebody to lean on
Fertilize the tree and keep the roots strong
Pikaninnie working the cotton field
Overseer said "I'll make you a good deal"
"If you work as hard as you work the field, in my house
The same food I eat will be in your mouth"
Little Hymie left his friends and family
And moved into a world of vanity
To end up in a state of insanity
They made him work real hard for the master
It was like a good life sentence, on and after
Clean linens, clean clothes and a fresh bath
Sometimes he gets so happy he just laughs
Not thinking about those he left behind
Picking cotton night and day eating nothing but swine
He even said he was better than the cotton picker
Because they call him by name and not little nigger
So he wondered what happened to the house nigger that worked before me
He must have worked so good that the master set him free
If I please my master maybe
I'll get my freedom card
The next time my master let me beat a slave
I'll whip him extra hard
So he whipped some and hung some from a tree
He said he will do anything for the dream of being free
The young brother didn't think about the law ofgravity
What goes up must come down
Or the three hundred and sixty degrees
What goes around comes around
Now years gone past, the house nigger is now an old man
The master said "I give him an order and he looks like he don't understand"
He's just old and worthless like a fruit gone rotten
So the master ordered the house nigger back to picking cotton
Back on the fields where he started from
He looked for his friends but he had none
When he died he left as an old lonely man
Someone who forgot he was and African
All he wanted was to succeed, he didn't mean no harm
Institutionalized by an oppressed system he became an Uncle Tom
The moral to this story is plain
It's OK to climb the ladder but don't forget from where you came

MY SHADOW, MY SON

I see you following me
Doing the things that I do
Science would say it's impossible
For me to follow you
There's light within your mist
We can't go on without the light
Living in a wicked world
Living in darkness
Travel with me, move within motion
Feel the vibrations, sense my emotion
Speak to me, I know you know
Follow me, feel my soul
There you are wherever I go
Me and my shadow
Me and my shadow
One times one plus one
The only one that's true
The only one I trust
One times one, is one, plus one, is two
Who else besides me, besides my shadow
My son.

ENJOYING MY FAMILY
IN A PEACEFUL WAY

I woke this morning in"a peaceful way
Said my prayers, had a coffee, and started
Off my day

Got into my car and started off to work
Someone had road rage flipped me the finger
And called me a jerk

I broke down on the highway with a broken fan belt
For two hours I sat there waiting for some help
So I walked two miles to a gas station
They didn't believe me when I explained
My situation

Finally I got a tow truck to take me on my way
They wanted to see my 10 to make sure I
Wasn't stealing someone else's triple A

I got my car fixed and started off again
And then I got pulled over by a police man

He wanted to know what I was doing in that neighborhood
Treated me like a thief that was
Up to no good

He gave me a sobriety test
Put me in hand cuffs like I was under arrest

He called my name in for warrants and then let
Me go
Then he warned me to be cautious and drive slow

I stopped at the store for some chewing gum
Everyone was staring at me
Like I had a gun
Security was following me around the store
Like I was the enemy, and we was in a silent war

Finally I made it to work, late for the first time
My boss is screaming and was going out of his mind

Threatened to fire me if I was late again
And this is when all my problems at work begin

Some co-workers act high sidity
Others are just raunchy
And two faced, and to damn pretty

Some smile in your face, and stab you in the back
Some don't say nothing cause they don't like blacks
Some are soft and understanding
And some are just too hard
I want to pack up and quit,
But I need this job

Because times are hard
My boss is crazy
The guy that works with me is so damn lazy
He sits around all day drinking coffee and tea
Thinking all the work should be done by me

I got a house full of kids
I need food for the fridge
I got a lot of bills to pay
So I held my pride and made
It through the day

I went home to my wife and kids
And looking at there faces, gives me the strength
To live
In a world thats corrupt, and full of so much stress
We still have each other, never the less
And in spite of all my problems
I finished my day
Enjoying my family
In a peaceful way

A JACK IN A BOX

I must have passed out last night
Man I had the weirdest dream
All I remember is leaving that wild party at my boy jays house
My wife didn't even know where I was at
Man we had a lot to drink at that party
I remember leaving the house and walking to my car,
That's all I remember
Man did we have fun;
I don't know what they put in that punch
But it got me wasted
I must still be dreaming, what is this room I'm in
Look their goes all of my family
All of my uncles and aunts, my brothers, most of my friends;
Man everyone is here
Look there goes my mother and my father;
It's been a long time since I saw them together
There all sitting down, it looks like there in church, someone must be getting married
Hay there goes my wife, and my children, why is my mother and wife hugging and crying
Why do all of my children look so sad and confused?
Hay who is this preacher, I never saw him before
Now everyone is crying
Owe that's so nice everyone is getting up, one at a time, and saying some nice things
about someone, they keep calling him he
He left a wife and children, he made a bad choice
I wonder who they're talking about
Now they're getting up and there walking toward me
Why is everyone looking at me like that?
Look at all those pretty flowers
My mom is touching my face, but I don't feel anything
Here is my loving wife
Hold up baby, it's me jack, what are you doing, don't close this box
I can't see anything
Don't leave me locked up in this box
Where is every one, somebody
Help me I can't breathe
I feel so tied I am going to sleep, I can't fight it, somebody please
, Help me help me. It's me its jack
I'm right here
Get me out of this box

A JACK IN THE BOX

TO A CHILD WHO LIVES ALONE

Have you ever been so lonely that you felt that no one cared?
Did you ever feel like crying, but new you'd get know were
Have you ever wondered God why me, ' why me'
Have you ever tried to imagine; even hallucinate, just to escape reality
Know body hears your cry, know body knows your pain
Have you ever lived with a bunch of strangers, who barely know your name?
Have you ever had to pray, God give me a home
I have no mommy or know daddy and I am so alone
Have you ever contemplated suicide just to get someone to listen?
Have you ever acted out in anger just to get attention?
Have you ever had to wonder, what does my mom look like
I wish I had a dad to teach me how to ride a bike
If you have never felt these things, God has smiled your way
Because there are children who feel these pains every single day
Have you ever thought about sharing some of your wealth?
Have you ever thought that God has blessed you, so you can be a blessing to someone else?
Have you ever thought about adopting to make your house a home?
To give a hug, and show some love to a child who lives alone

I JUST WANT TO BE FREE

Till death do us part?
You are my heart
When will this dream end?

When he came into her life
It was all sugar and spice
Lovers and best friends

A few months gone passed
What she thought would last
Only faded away

Mistreating and beating
Used and abused
Unable to run away
And forced to stay,

What friends and family see
Is Love and unity, peace and tranquility
And know body knows that you're living a lie
You don't know what to do
Or who you can explain this to
How did you get such a big black eye?

I met a woman today who tried to run away
She said I have taken all I can take

She said my husband's always angry
Battering and beating me
I want to be free
But I stay for the children's sake

First it was like a dream
Then he became so mean
Selfish and unfair

I wish I can run and hide
I even thought about suicide
Because my life has become a living nightmare

I met a kid in fear, had a face full of tears
He said his mother just died'
He ask me for bail because daddies in jail, something about a homicide,

A man is someone who respects his wife
And for his family he will sacrifice
Even his own life

A Man seeks peace and let live
Loves and forgives

Where can you go when your brought so low, with loneliness and despair
You try so hard even pray to god, and it seems like your get know were
By hiding the lies you to can die
So wake up and smell the coffee
For it is a crime and he can do time
For assault and battery

What kind of man spends his life?
Scaring his children and beating his wife
Going out and getting drunk
When His drinking buddies treat him like a punk
He goes home frustrated and mad
And treats his wife like a punching bag
A vicious cycle over again
She tries to fight back but just can't win
And he feels like one heck of a guy
But you never miss your water till the well runs dry
Now she's gone and you're all alone
She gets the car the kids and the home
The only time you see her is in family court
Because she needs more child support
And now your crying how can she do this to me
Remember the ASSAULT AND BATTERY

You never thought of the ripple affect
The things that your children will never forget
Or they may think that it's ok
For men to treat women that violent way
A split family and broken home
To know that mommy is all alone
And daddy is somewhere in jail
Begging a judge to reduce his bail
Praying to god, please don't let them convict me
To Domestic violence and ASSAULT AND BATTERY
I JUST WANT TO BE FREE
I JUST WANT TO BE FREE

AND THE DOOR SHALL BE OPEN

My life has always been a constant struggle
Standing on unstable ground
There's always someone judging me
Taking my past and putting me down
Live and let live
Focus on your self
Stop hiding your faults by focusing on someone ells
A dog that will bring you a bone will carry one
If you listen to someone talk about the next man, and what he do
Then that same one won't have no problem talking about you
When you change the way you look at people
The people you look at will change
Change your Attitude
See one can find fault in anyone
You will find what you seek after

You look for hate you'll find tears
You look for love peace and laughter

And the door shall be open unto you

I live in a world of constant stereotype
Where everything is black
Where everything is white
What difference does it make?
It's just the color of one's skin
, Dogs come in all different colors and there still dogs
Yet we can't just be men
Amongst men
Because of the color of our skin
Change your Attitude
And the door shall be open UN to you

Spiritually dead
Living in darkness
Claiming to have the light
Ignorance comes in all nationalities
In this world of the constant stereotype
The man who sees his faults and refuses to correct them
Is a fool?
The wise man sees his faults and corrects them
With a godly attitude
And the door shall be open unto you

VOICE FROM A PRISON CELL
I AM ALREADY DEAD'

from the pains of a baby born

to the lynching of a man scorn

a life spent dodging the penitentiary
constantly, constantly

trying to unite with the white inside of me
dreaming for a better life, forced to except whatever may be
in my mind, all the time of prison bars
the way the devil used me
live this way or die
naturally I, seek to be free
so I rejected a system that abused me

yet it is not I, who holds the key
the key of life, my destiny
the shackles of pain and poverty
lord have mercy

so I fantasize with the lies, that I can be part of the American dream
dream
dreaming keeps me alive
I even fantasize

can I turn back the hands of time
and correct a young distorted angry mind
the flesh fulfills me with so much pleasure
pleasure that makes me want to live forever
so I dream

if my life was a movie
would it be a documentary of my reality of struggle
or a autobiography of constant trouble

so I look into the sky and ask God' why'
why me?
how come I can't break free
from what i am, that imprisons me

why am I living in hell
looking to heaven
in a world that's so unfair
I want to live in heaven to
but why I got to die to get there

here I stand as a man, hated in a world I am in
trapped within my rejected skin, my rejected skin

many years I sat in this cadge
all my life I suffered and aged

the living dead, looking into the sky
confusion remains in my eyes

some hear me, some fear me, everyone judges me
some hate me, some debate me, some even say they love me

my world is so much more, full of war, and blood shed
you won't give, nor let me live, so I am already dead

I fight a war, my forefather fought for, and I can never win
I been miss judged, and shown no love, because of the skin I am in
the skin I am in

I am a slave, who lives in a grave, called the penitentiary
I look into the sky, were jail bird fly, dreaming to be free

everyday people die, and never make the news paper
I pray to live long enough just to open my own refrigerator

ill rather have, the mental block, of fools rules laws and fear
then to crawl, behind these walls, with a face full of tears

I humbly bow before you, with water in my eyes
wily lynch you smell of stench, but I'll live your way or die

you beat me down, and took my crown, and burnt down my thrown
you worked real hard to give me your God, and still I am left alone
you rule my life in front of my wife who calls me her head
there's no more you can do to me, cause, I AM ALREADY DEAD

REMINDED BY A RAINBOW

I've heard many songs
I've read many poems
My sunshine and my storms
This morning was kind of dreary
As I gazed upon the dew
And then I saw a rainbow
That's when I thought of you.

Your eyes are like the stars
As they glitter through the night
Your teeth are like the clouds
So pure and pearly white
Your love reminds me of the sky
So strong, so soft, so blue
And when I see a rainbow
I'll always think: of you.

I AM-
A 'MAN'

excuse me
while i release some stress
put my hand to my chess
and take a deep breath
because we still struggle
and yet still blessed
let me take your mind
back to a time
of the klu klux klan
a brother was walking the set
with a sigh on his neck
with these 4 words,
I-AM -A-MAN
the mother land is Africa
the land of which, the human race came from
if the first man, came from Africa
then why i got to prove to you
that- j. am- one
you went to Africa
and captured a' African 'MAN'
bought him to a foreign land
like a terrorist
beet him, and mistreat him
and made him exist
with racism
and prejudice
you took his pride
his religion
and corrupted his brain
raped his mother
killed his brother
disgraced his father
and changed his name
and to this day we live a this way,
seeking to be free
free from unfairness
and careless
hate and slavery
tell me, if I work and, pay taxes,
the system will work for me
now how can i support a system,
with no racial equality

this land is your land, this land is my land
from California, to the new York island
a song they taught us in middle school
why should i listen to the politician
who promised me forty acres and a mule

so we work from sun up to sun down,
while you lived large and free
in this country
tis of thee
sweet land of liberty
and now you call me' crazy
uneducated and lazy
a good canadate for, social security
then- you -do- all -you- can
to -prove- that- i am,
less- than
A-MAN
wIth political shackles, and invisible chains
with the epidemic of dope, and crack cocaine, on my brain
and in my neighborhood
wile you smoke weed in the suburb,
living lavishly and good
excuse me
while i release some stress
put my hand to my chess
and take a deep breath
because we still struggle
and yet still blessed
yes we shall over come
from this day forth and after,
in a country that looks down on me,
were the slave becomes the master
you filled graves with slaves
who wanted to read and right
and now we stand, American,
ready to fight for our rights
you say know more civil rights war
yet set trap, to keep us out
so martin Luther king took the peaceful rout
we've been sprayed by water hoses,
bit by your dogs
knocked down, but not knocked out
every race you met, you brutally defeated
raped robbed, miss treated and beaten
you are the swine of the world

brought greed to the nation
can't even sit in the sun to long
what they call it,
'pigmentation'
you ate the good part of the pig,
and gave us the intestines, full of shit
we looked in your face
said our grace
and made a, meal out of it
after scrubbing your f1oors, on all four's
and cleaning your nasty house

after raising your little children
black nigger, still came out of there filthy mouth
now we got a black president
in the' white' house
cleaning house once again
cleaning up your money brackets
with political tickets
war, and all that other shit you got us in
you claim it wasn't you
but it was your fore fathers who
spread hate that killed off nations
and all, bad habits
have been
passed down through generations
the world's biggest 'hypocrite',
baptized in lies
sits in church, with the Madonna
surrounded by manmade saints
waving a fan
then all week, you lie and cheat
and take your aggressions out on the black man
you treat us like animals, and tell us we got rights
like the right to remain silent
while you use us, and abuse us
and great us with violence
treat us like we the enemy
of this country
when we built the foundation of this land
then deprive me
from all my capabilities
and tell me i ant no' man'
while turning down your face
on the black race,
like your shit smell so good
just by my presents
i am the mere essence
of your Livelihood

and to this day, we live this way
seeking to be free
free from unfairness
and carless
hate and slavery
excuse me
while i release some stress
put my hand to my chess
and take a deep breath
because we still struggle
and yet still blessed
the things you did to the black women
no other human being could endure
you took blood from a blessed one

mixed it and made it un pure
'know', were not human
we are, animals,
black and ungodly, with the devils eye
what kind of a man would rape a animal
hate and have a baby bye
and still the back women gives the family
all the love and strength in their heart
the ones you murdered, sold off,
tide to horses and pulled apart
they cook, they clean, and take the burdens, and pains
that, you inflict on their man
for over, four hundred and thirty five years of generations
we still feel the pinch
we still smell the stench
of the dead body's
diabolically strategized by
wily lynch
my black queens have gods strength
and the faith of Abraham
without the spirit of the sisters,
you wouldn't have no land
or the black, ' MAN, '
and when you treat us with hate
she's the only one, who understands
that even though
you treat me less than
I am,
still a man
ma ma held her little baby
she had big dreams for us

not probation,
not the police station
or sitting on the back of the bus
slavery days ant over
the strategy just changed
political chains and poor people campaigns
they just revised the names
like nigger, negro, "BLACK"
hymie, Piccananny, jigger boo
everything but a man
can't even call us striate out,
American'
excuse me
while i release some stress
put my hand to my chess
and take a deep breath
because we still struggle
and yet still blessed
i want the privileges you got
but i cant be like you

'evil' sinful, criminal
can my children live in peace to
like you do
in a good neighborhood
were they won't live in fright
constantly fighting for what's right
or dying every night
were Liquor stores, ain't on every block
we're a young black men, don't die,
from a gunshot,
of a racist cop
I am
am the style that your children imatate
the main focus at a political dibate
i- am the blessing, that allows you to be blessed
the back you stand on for rest
the Malcolm x, and martin Luther king
and you treat me and beat me
remember, Rodney king
i am the man you dream to be
i am your sanity
where would you be, without me?
i -am the object that you market
the government pays the state,
and fills the white collar, pocket
i am human real-estate

yes the inmate
paid for by the state
to keep me confined, and blind, doing time, 'all the time'
behind
the prison walls
out of sight and out of mind
I am
your spiritual force
your life source
you have stole my music and talents, and took the credit
i- am the originator
not the duplicator,
and don't you ever forget it
i- am created in the image of my creator
i- am a descended of kings
there for' i am
ME
and meant to be
'royalty'
and like a' God', i walk with wisdom
my creator is constantly in my heart,
and my thoughts are from him
I fight, like king David,
I m wise, like king Solomon
I am

the seed, that made this country grow
I- am the back breaking money making super man
and the next time you try to kill me
just know that, 'indestructible'
'I AM'
my culture was stolen,
and yet i am still rooted from a strong tree
I AM, i am, a man
a man, i am "HE"
he who is dark, and gives light,
and spiritual insight
he who die's and multiplies
he who opens mankind's eyes
right on, can you dig it,
and that ant no' white mans, jive'
you took my style, and racial profile
manipulated, and duplicated
and made millions off of me
and i shall still thrive to stay alive
like the roots
from my family tree
wisdom should tell you
don't make me suffer no longer
cause that which doesn't kill me
only makes me stronger

why am I so angry
hungry for unity
and racial equality
can't you see
i live in a nation that thrives off my missary
they said join the army and be all i can be
to kill people of color that look like me
to come back home and still be
a NIGGAR, a REFUGEE
a second class citizen,
on a land built by my family
a system that enslaved me
talking about saving me
from what?
who is my enemy
excuse me
while i release some stress
put my hand to my chess
and take a deep breath
because we still struggle
and yet still blessed
so i asked God
why our life got to be
so hard
why we got to die to have our heaven
while there's is here on earth

then god told me, all the earthy positions ant nothing
compared to what heavens worth
see Satan exist through prejudice
he uses every one
it's not the white man
that you fight man
even he can be my son
put your faith in the right place
for the wages of sin is death
you just live in love and peace
and let me do the rest
see i am a merciful God
full of love and full of grace
and i invite all to come
regardless of sex or race
so don't be swayed by the devil
the truth he will never understand
when i created you in my image
the master had a master plan

you ask why you seem to suffer
while everyone ells have fun
can't you see, your meant to be
the heavenly chosen one
my best work of art
you don't shine
for what's in your mind
but for what's in your heart
the slaves that filled the graves
will one day be restored
for they will be the ones
who comes with my son
and win the mighty war
and before your eyes
the dead will rise
and sin will be no more
so don't hold no grudge
and don't miss judge
but do the best you can
for when I looked down
and took up the ground
I created a man

and to this, day i pray
to walk a righteous way
on this God given land
that I can live
love and forgive
because, the I am
I-AM
A-MAN

Bull whip and beat a slave
Willy lynched in diabolical ways
Of weakening the mind
And strengthening the body
We suffer we feel pain
Yet never die
That which doesn't kill me
Only makes me stronger
I live through my children
Therefore I live
Through generations of myself
God is the power that shapes my way
There for my feet are set on a path
That 'I' may follow